Endorse

What a gem! There's so muc
tips included in this book. Working in change management
and strategy, it's all about getting people to act differently,
which is incredibly hard. To act differently, you need to feel
differently, and to do that, we must think differently. That's
where hope comes in. I've used the Hope Playsheet from
Ian for many years, and seen firsthand how it has radically
changed the mindset, motivations, and outcomes for many
people while positively impacting workplace culture.

As someone who loves to understand the context of subject
matter, this book was an exploration of the wider history,
cultures, application and impact of hope. Words have impact
and this is a reclamation of one of our most powerful words
at hand.

Every leader, manager, parent, or friend can use this method
to help coach and care for others. Hope is teachable, and
hope is learnable; this book will guide you through both,
making hope a natural part of your process. And, I love
how this book can positively impact not just our working
lives, but every aspect of life, enabling us to live richer, more
fulfilling lives.

Catrin Lewis, Founder, Cultures That Pop

I know that hope isn't just a feeling, it's the spark that drives
action, sustains resilience, and fuels the fight for justice.
Ian Pettigrew understands this deeply. In *Hope is a Strategy*,

he not only explores the power of fostering hope through the patterns and ideas but gives readers practical ways to cultivate Hope in even the hardest of seasons.

This is a book that will help all leaders or aspiring leaders who are looking to demonstrate realistic optimism and effective leadership.

Ian's support on our international board and with our staff teams in Ethiopia and Uganda has shown me the impact of his words in action; his coaching brings strength and encouragement to those working on the frontlines of complex, emotionally demanding work. This book is an extension of that same generosity and wisdom.

I am very grateful for Ian and the time he has taken to invest in others by writing this book. It's timely, grounded, and beautifully written. Whether you're leading a team, navigating uncertainty, or simply trying to move forward, *Hope is a Strategy* offers both inspiration and a path to follow.

Tim Nelson, CEO, Hope for Justice

As a beacon of positivity Ian has always shared and inspired hope with those he meets. Here, in this book, he explains how you can understand, develop, and build on your skills as a leader to learn, and teach hope and trust. A book that has arrived when it's so important to choose hope.

Sara Nelson, Programme Director,
DigitalHealth.London

Things are better when we choose hope. Hope is a strategy. I believe this in my heart. Ian, through his warmth, generosity of spirit, and beautiful writing takes us on a journey to truly understand what hope is and isn't, how to encourage ourselves and others to find it and most importantly a structure to enable all of us to be more intentional about the role of hope in our daily lives – at work, at home, in our communities and in the world! In particular for me, is how hope shows up in the workplace and I love that this can help leaders at all levels to develop hope as a strategy in their daily practices. Hope can and will change the world!

Dawn Smedley, Founder and
Host of the Culture Whisperer Podcast

I first met Ian at an airport in Dubai on the way to Uganda for a skills-based volunteering trip to work with the staff of a charity called Hope for Justice. The next day, along with a third musketeer, we were asked to deliver a workshop on goal-setting. We hoped it would work well, but what initially seemed like a simple workshop evolved into a workshop on hope and was hugely impactful for all involved.

Ian, his work, and this book, are symbols of hope that come at a much-needed time. Negativity is rising, toxic positivity is rife, isolation and disconnection are growing rapidly, and something needs to close the gap, to not just bring us back together, but to pull us back together, and *Hope is a Strategy* can do just that.

Ian has an ability to beautifully combine research, play, academia, and the human touch in all that he does, and he's captured all of this beautifully in his first (of many?) books.

Hope is a Strategy can help to take that niggle of hope that you have telling you that things will get better, and show you how to take that hope, and turn it into something tangible. This is a must read for every leader, especially those who are hopeful about a changing future for the world of work. Read this book and then take the learnings and make hope happen!

Kelly Swingler, The Burnoutologist, Burnout Survivor, Global Burnout Educator, TEDx Speaker, Author

Hope is a Strategy is needed now more than ever. It's both profound and practical and serves as a great reminder that when we focus on hope, we can create a better future for ourselves and others. Ian writes beautifully, bringing both a full heart and deep knowledge to the subject, as he shares his inspiring personal stories, coaching wisdom, and extensive research.

Highlighting the importance of belief, trust and the power of coaching, this book felt like a conversation with a friend, the kind who won't let you give up, even when you want to. Above all, Ian's words encourage us to believe that we can influence what comes next in our lives.

This book is highly practical and provides us with tools and techniques to inspire hope. I particularly love the Hope Playsheet, a new way to self-coach, combining hope, and inspired action.

Whether you're navigating personal change, leading a team or hoping to make your mark on the world, this book is a must read. And if you've ever been tempted to give up, this book will stop you in your tracks and remind you that hope really is a choice and a very powerful strategy.

Jo Wright, Co-founder of Coaching Culture, Author of *No More Sh*t Managers*

HOPE
IS A STRATEGY

**Why realistic optimism is essential
for effective leadership**

Ian B. Pettigrew

First published in Great Britain by Practical Inspiration Publishing, 2026

ISBN   978-1-78860-660-8 (hardback)
        978-1-78860-661-5 (paperback)
        978-1-78860-663-9 (epub)

EU GPSR representative: LOGOS EUROPE, 9 rue Nicolas Poussin, LA ROCHELLE 17000, France Contact@logoseurope.eu

Want to bulk-buy copies of this book for your team and colleagues? We can customize the content and co-brand *Hope is a Strategy* to suit your business's needs.

Please email info@practicalinspiration.com for more details.

Contents

Part 1

Hope 101

1

How to use this book

First, there is a companion website to the book that you can find at https://hope.tips where you will find a downloadable copy of the Hope Playsheet and lots of additional resources, videos, and interviews with people about their hope journeys.

You are the expert in you

Hope often gets wrongly confused with wishful thinking which leads people to say that hope is not a strategy. We'll be diving really deep into the concept of hope throughout this book but, for now, let's just say that hope is a really active pursuit of a better future and is definitely not wishful thinking. Hope can transform lives, fuel dreams, and provide the strength to overcome the toughest challenges. I've been fortunate to spend a significant part of my life immersed in the study and application of hope, both through my professional work and academic research. Over the years, I've learned a great deal about what hope means, how it can be cultivated, and the profound impact it can have on our lives. I firmly believe that hope is a strategy.

In my journey, I've discovered what works for me and have had the privilege of helping others find hope in their own lives. However, there's an important truth I've come to understand; neither I nor anyone else can be the expert on your life. You are the expert in you. This realization is at the heart of everything I share in my work.

Through my experiences, I've identified certain patterns and ideas that generally work in fostering hope. These are strategies that have proven effective for many people, including myself. They are the building blocks of hope, the steppingstones that can lead to a more hopeful and fulfilling life. But remember, these are just patterns. They are guidelines that might resonate with you.

While these patterns are valuable, it's crucial to recognize that you hold the key to your own hope. You are the expert in your life, and only you can determine what truly works for you. This means evaluating each idea, each strategy, and each pattern to see how it fits into your unique life story. It's about taking ownership of your journey and crafting a path that aligns with your personal values and aspirations.

As we explore the concept of hope, please try to approach it with openness. Be willing to experiment, to try new things, and to learn from your experiences. Understand that what works for one person may not work for another, and that's perfectly okay. Your journey is uniquely yours, and it's up to you to navigate it with courage and self-awareness.

Experiment and reflect

Sometimes in psychology I think we delude ourselves that we know the answers and I think we feel professional pressure to do so. If I were coaching you on finding hope, I'd probably have loads of ideas for any challenge you mention. Whilst I'd be encouraging you to come up with your own ideas, in the back of my mind I'd have a ton of ideas for things that might work. They'd be a mixture of things that have worked for me, things that have worked for other clients, things that I know from research, and a whole load of hypotheses and hunches.

For any situation where we want to build hope, there will be loads of ideas. Some of which will work, and some of which might have no effect or even make things worse. You might be able to quickly identify what will work for you based on previous experiences, or you may not. You might be left with a whole host of ideas that could work and the only way to identify the ones that work is to actually try them. That could take a long time but there are ways that you can accelerate the process.

Eric Ries[1] tells a story of how he founded a business, secured funding, and then spent months alongside his team developing a platform that would allow college students to create profiles that companies could then view as part of their recruitment process. They built a fantastic feature-rich platform that they were proud of. Only to find out that there wasn't a market for what they were creating because nobody wanted to use it. That's a very expensive way to discover the answer to the question 'is there a market for this thing?'. On reflection, Ries realized that they could have answered that question by either creating a one-page landing page and tracking sign-ups expressing interest in a forthcoming service, or even conducted some interviews to test the assumptions. Ries writes extensively about testing a 'minimum viable product', and about validating learning and iterating. Ries's approach encourages us not to make assumptions about what will work, but to look for the cheapest, easiest, scrappiest way to answer the

---

[1] Ries, E. (2011). *The Lean Startup*. Portfolio Penguin.

questions about what will work. Sometimes we need to pick the things that look most likely to work and then conduct a series of simple experiments. Mock it up or pretend and give something a go for a couple of weeks. If it works, stick with it. If it doesn't, then you've got some learning, and you can try something else.

The newly-published book *Tiny Experiments* by Anne-Laure Le Cunff[2] explores the whole concept of conducting these little experiments as Anne-Laure has been 'working out loud' in the writing of the book. Le Cunff ran a whole series of tiny experiments such as testing alternative book titles (seeing how people responded in person to mentions of the book title and running online ads with different titles). This whole concept of an experimental mindset can be applied in so many domains and encourages us not to guess when we don't know something, but to run a tiny experiment to find out.

Dr Stuart Eglin has written an excellent book, *Precious Jewels: Small experiments for personal growth*[3] about how he runs small experiments, reflecting on 24 experiments that he's run to help him with either focus, purpose, or creativity. I'm going to

[2] Le Cunff, A.-L. (2025). *Tiny Experiments*. Penguin.
[3] Eglin, S. (2025). *Precious Jewels: Small experiments for personal growth*. Bluewater Books.

confess straight away that Stuart was kind enough to include me in the acknowledgements section as I was his coach for a few years, and he mentions that the idea of small experiments arose from a coaching session. With that disclaimer aside, it is an excellent book and it is a delight to get an inside look at personal experiments, although Stuart took it one stage further and ran the writing of the book itself as an experiment!

I do hope that this book will help you find lots of ideas, but please do think about what experiments you can run to test them and find the best ones for you.

Small steps

We've all heard the sayings: 'Nothing grows in your comfort zone', or 'Life begins at the end of your comfort zone'. These motivational quotes urge us to step out of our familiar spaces and into the unknown. While there can be truth in these words, it's crucial to understand the balance between comfort and discomfort. The Yerkes-Dodson[4] curve, a performance model, has sometimes been applied to suggest that we need more pressure to increase performance, something that isn't always true. The

---

[4] https://simplypsychology.org/what-is-the-yerkes-dodson-law.html

classic normal distribution (or bell curve) shows that performance increases as pressure increases, up to a point. Beyond that, increased pressure results in a deterioration in performance. If you're under no pressure and are bored, then increased pressure might increase your performance. If you're already under loads of pressure and struggling, then increased pressure might only serve to make things worse.

So, where do we find the optimal space for growth? Enter the stretch zone. In 2006, Ryan and Markova introduced a model[5] that categorizes our learning experiences into three zones: the comfort zone, the stretch zone, and the panic zone. The comfort zone is where we feel safe and secure, but it's also where growth is minimal. On the other hand, the panic zone is where challenges become overwhelming, leading to stress and fear that can paralyse us. The key is to find a balance between these extremes.

While some advocate for bold actions and stepping into the unknown, the panic zone can be counterproductive. When we're too far out of our comfort zone, fear and stress can consume us, triggering a fight-or-flight response. This state is not conducive to learning or growth, as our energy is

---

[5] https://commonslibrary.org/the-learning-zone-model/

spent managing panic rather than embracing new experiences. It's a place we should avoid lingering in for too long.

The stretch zone is the sweet spot for growth. Here, we push our boundaries and explore new possibilities without feeling overwhelmed. It's a space where things feel unfamiliar, yet manageable. We have a safety net, allowing us to take calculated risks and learn from them. In the stretch zone, we can experiment, innovate, and truly grow.

To thrive in the stretch zone, start by taking small steps. Gradually push yourself beyond your comfort zone, but not so far that you enter the panic zone. Try new things, test new possibilities, and allow yourself to feel a bit uncomfortable. This is where real learning happens. By consistently operating in the stretch zone, you might find yourself growing in ways you never imagined.

It might take a bit of thinking to find the balance, but there is huge value to be gained. I feel this all the time in my Everesting training; whilst my natural instinct of 'if some is good then more is better' drives me to train really hard and stretch myself all the time, I've learned (the hard way) that is also where burnout lies and now I've found this very attractive middle ground where I stretch, but not break, myself.

There's another reason to take smaller steps and avoid wading straight into the panic zone. Barbara Fredrickson's work on 'broaden and build theory'[6] suggests that our emotions – the way we feel about a challenge – changes the way we engage with it. If we are far out of our comfort zone, negative emotions such as fear will narrow the range of options we believe are available to us. For example, If I were facilitating an interactive workshop with a large group of hundreds of people and felt fearful of it failing, I'm not going to be at my most creative. I'd be unlikely to experiment and try new approaches such as an unconference. (An unconference is an approach where the participants co-create the agenda for the conference, on the day. So, you don't know exactly what is going to crop up. Exciting, powerful, and scary!) Rather, the fear would probably result in me preparing loads of slides and sticking to a script. The negative emotion of fear restricts my thinking. In contrast, imagine I'm in my comfort zone by working with a group of six people. I feel positive about it and I have a whole range of positive emotions (maybe excitement and curiosity) when I come to work with them. Those positive emotions broaden the range of options I believe are available to me and result in me being prepared to try new things

---

[6] https://pmc.ncbi.nlm.nih.gov/articles/PMC1693418/

and experiment. The key question in this scenario is how do I progress from working with six people to working with hundreds of people. The answer is gradually and with small steps. If I volunteer to lead a workshop with eight or ten people then it will likely feel like a bit of a stretch, but I can still lean into those positive emotions and do it well. At the end of the workshop, I've also learned that I can work with a bigger group. That learning gives me a coping resource, the knowledge that I can do more. Leaning into that and taking small steps to increasingly work with larger groups would get me to where I want to get to.

When we hope for something radically different to what we have today, we might feel that we need to take massive scary, bold steps. Maybe. Or maybe we can consistently take smaller steps and keep pushing our stretch zone. Again, you are the expert in you.

Hope starts with you

I've written this book with leaders in mind, exploring why realistic optimism is essential for effective leadership. Leadership can show up in many domains and you might have a role and job title that says you are a leader, or you may not. Alternatively, you might be an aspiring leader or you might be using your leadership skills in a social group, your family, a church, a charity, or any other domain. You don't have to have the job title to get value from this book, but much of the content is about how to help other people to find hope.

But before we explore how to help other people find hope, we need to find it ourselves. Leading by example is powerful so if you want to help other people find hope, it starts with you. Part 1 of this book explores what hope is and isn't, before exploring a brief history of hope and how it is viewed within some of the world's major religions. Part 2 of this book is focused on you and how you can find and sustain hope for yourself, which sets the foundation for Part 3 where we'll look at how you can be a 'Hopeful leader' and help other people to find hope through realistic optimism.

2

Reclaiming hope

What is hope?

We'll dive deep into what we really mean by hope later on, but for now let's simply say that it has just three components; a belief that things will be better than they are now, a belief that we can do what it takes to make that a reality, and the ability to navigate the bumps in the journey that life inevitably throws our way. That's it. Hope is what helps us focus on how we want things to be and helps us get there. Without hope, we stay where we are. Hope is visionary, active, scrappy, and resourceful.

If I make this personal for a moment, hope has played a big part in my life. After breaking all three bones in my ankle (a trimalleolar fracture) I announced that I was going to complete a cycling 'Everesting' challenge, an endurance cycling challenge that entails repeating hill climbs until you have ascended the height of Everest (29,029 feet). For me, I know that this is a similar challenge to completing four marathons back-to-back in one day. At the time of writing, my training is going well. By the time of publication, I 'hope' to have completed it. When I cross the finish line on that challenge, it will be hope that got me over that line. It will be the vision and desire. It will be the hours of training but more than anything, it will be the way that I have navigated the bumps in the road. It will be the way that I have dealt with external challenges like illness, business travel taking me away from home, family issues, and the biggest challenge of all: me when I get in my own way. I'll share more about Everesting in Chapter 11.

This book itself has been a journey of hope; I am not at all a natural writer, finding it to be one of the most difficult things I do. Despite that, I'd long harboured an ambition to write a book on hope. An ambition that simply frustrated me because it remained unfulfilled and felt, perhaps paradoxically, hopeless. In order to confirm my decision to abandon the ambition, I went on a writing workshop with Alison Jones and Bec Evans and well, here we are. The research for and the writing of this book have been some of the most difficult things I have ever done in my 50+ years on this planet. If you are reading these words, it is hope that got them to you.

Again, hope is visionary, active, scrappy, and resourceful. But we get sloppy with the way that we use the word in everyday conversations; 'I hope this email finds you well', 'I hope that my (football) team win the Premier League', 'I'm hoping that things will turn out OK at work', 'I'm hopeful for the future'. If we tried to reverse engineer the meaning of hope from everyday conversations, I suspect that we'd think it meant either wishing that something were true, or a general optimism about things getting better.

Henry Ford touched on hope when he said 'Whether you think you can or you think you can't, you're right', although I would argue that is an overly simplistic view on hope. Hope is common in everyday language, whether it be 'Hope is on the horizon', 'filled with hope', 'losing hope', or 'hanging onto hope'. Language matters and I often correct myself when I think I've been 'lucky' when I've achieved something that I've hoped for and worked really hard for. I try to use the word 'fortunate' instead, simply to acknowledge that we can sometimes do all the right things but not see the result. Achieving what we hope for isn't luck.

For now, let's explore three pieces of evidence about real hope.

1 Victor Frankl – *Man's Search for Meaning*[7]

This classic text on hope is an inspiring but difficult read, drawing on Frankl's own experience of enduring extreme suffering in a Nazi concentration camp. Frankl argues that hope arises from finding meaning in life, even in the most difficult of circumstances. Challenging though it seems, he asserts that we always retain the freedom to choose our attitude toward suffering so that we can always choose hope, even when we are in the most difficult circumstances beyond our control. Frankl talks about 'tragic optimism', about keeping hope and finding meaning in the most difficult of times. We'll return to the idea of never ever losing hope in Chapter 5.

2 Hope and cancer[8]

Whilst nobody claims that hope can cure cancer, recent studies have suggested that hope helps. There have been several studies that have measured hope in cancer patients alongside other psychological variables and then used hope interventions (to

---

[7] Frankl, V. E. (2006). *Man's Search for Meaning*. Beacon Press. (Original work published 1946.)

[8] Feldman, D. B., & Corn, B. W. (2023). Hope and cancer. *Current Opinion in Psychology*, 49, 101506. https://doi.org/10.1016/j.copsyc.2022.101506

increase hope) and examined the effects. Hope interventions with cancer patients have been found to reduce depression, increase a sense of coping, and support post-traumatic growth. There is some evidence that as a result of these things, people were living longer but there is a need for further robust research. In one study over a four-year period, people with high hope lived for a median of 15.93 months whilst people with low hope survived for 9.5 months. We need to be careful not to wildly extrapolate these results, but there is no doubt that hope is powerful. In these most challenging circumstances, it is important not to create false hope, but rather patients and their families wanted to hope for the best-case outcome but wanted to also know what the worst possible outcome was so they could prepare for it. We'll return to this theme of realistic optimism in Chapter 8 and several other times throughout the book. Finally, even when people were in end-of-life care, hope seems to help to reduce anxiety and depression.

3 Gallup's Global Leadership Report – what followers want[9]

Released in February 2025 at the World Governments Summit, Gallup's research explores what people

---

[9] www.gallup.com/analytics/656315/leadership-needs-of-followers. aspx

want from leaders and spans 52 countries, covering 76% of the world's adult population. Gallup's research found that people want four things from leaders; hope, trust, compassion, and stability. This comes as no surprise to me as this confirms Gallup's previous research over many years but one thing that stands out in this recent research is the importance of hope. Of the four needs, hope was the primary need, far outweighing all the others and ranking significantly higher than the second ranked need, trust. Hope gives people something to look forward to and helps them to navigate challenges whilst working towards a brighter future. Gallup found that where leaders provided hope, it increased thriving and reduced suffering and that hope was the leading need across all types of leaders (including education, organizational, political, religious, and family). Finally, the need for hope was mentioned more by younger people (aged 18–29 years) possibly reflecting the fact that people have their whole lives ahead of them and really value hope.

How we get hope so wrong?

Hope is a powerful force. It can transform our perspective, offering an empowering lens through which we can view challenges and envision the future. However, hope is often misunderstood. Our language can be imprecise, leading to hope being diluted into mere wishful thinking. It can sometimes resemble manifesting, where we focus solely on what we desire without considering the path to achieve it. This is a topic we'll explore further in Chapter 4.

Depending on their natural disposition, leaders may lean towards different approaches. Some naturally adopt a 'doom and gloom' mindset, convinced that nothing will work out. This pessimistic outlook doesn't work, as it fails to foster hope. On the opposite end of the spectrum lies toxic positivity, where one pretends everything will be fine, adopting a Pollyanna-like attitude. This approach is equally ineffective, as it often leads to disappointment and erodes trust. I've often seen this when we have a change of political leader where we swing between relentless optimism and doom and gloom. Neither work in isolation. The key lies in striking a balance and embracing realistic optimism. This middle ground acknowledges the challenges while maintaining a hopeful outlook. It is about being hopeful yet grounded, understanding that while things may not always go as planned, there is still potential for positive outcomes.

Hope is a valuable commodity. By nurturing it within ourselves and helping others to discover it, we can unlock a wealth of benefits. Realistic optimism empowers us to face challenges with resilience and determination, fostering a sense of trust and collaboration. As we navigate life's uncertainties, there's a real power from striving to cultivate hope and realistic optimism, creating a brighter future for ourselves and those around us.

A new language of hope

If we're going to get hope right, we need to be precise about the language we use. Whilst there aren't necessarily universally-accepted definitions of these words, I offer Figure 1 as a way of making sense of some related topics.

In Figure 1, I've shown **hope** as being the combination of both having a vision for the future and taking the action to make it a reality.

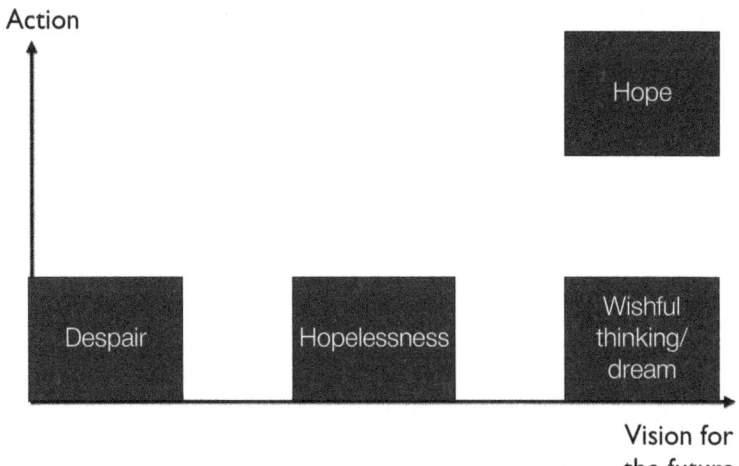

Figure 1 What is hope?

In contrast, **Wishful thinking** or a **Dream** involves having a vision for the future but not taking the action to make it a reality. What starts as hope could also turn into wishful thinking if we start to take action but then, for some reason, give up and stop taking action. More on this later.

Hopelessness is that state where we don't even dare to dream. Maybe we've been hopeful about something and it hasn't worked out so now we feel hopeless. Maybe that has happened in one domain of our live and we've had a kind of cross-contamination where the hopelessness spreads from one domain to another. Regardless of the cause, hopelessness keeps us stuck. It stops us dreaming of better, stops us taking action, and puts us at the mercy of our circumstances and external factors.

In contrast to hopelessness, a state of **despair** is even worse. Rather than be ambivalent or neutral about the future, we might catastrophize and imagine things (possibly everything) being worse.

Much of this book is about how to remain in the state of hope rather than the other options. If we're going to focus on hope then we need to use the word correctly, so let's explore some examples:

- I keep saying that I hope that Liverpool (other football teams are available) win the league this year. Does this pass the test of being a future vision of a better future? I believe so, although I know that fans of other teams will have other opinions. But now for the difficult question; can I take action to make this a reality? I could argue that I can sing at the top of my voice from the Sir Kenny Dalglish stand to encourage the team at home games, but I think the connection is tenuous and I can't actually influence the outcome of the Premier League. To be correct, I wish that Liverpool win the league but to say I hope is mis-using the word.

- I hope to complete the Everesting cycling challenge this year. Training for this challenge is really building my fitness and I'm doing it to raise money for a charity I care deeply about (Hope for Justice) so it is definitely a future vision of a better future. And I'm most definitely taking the action to make this a reality; I'm following a training plan and I am being very disciplined in executing the plan and cycling for typically six to nine hours of structured training each week. I'm being equally disciplined about nutrition, rest, and sleep so I feel like I'm taking all the action I need. Lots of things have already gotten in the way and I've navigated around them, as I will continue to for future challenges. Is it possible that something could happen that would either stop me doing it this year or stop me doing it at all? Of course it is, but I'm doing everything I can to create a successful outcome. That is hope.

- This is deeply personal but as I write this today, I've had some blood test results back with elevated PSA levels which might (but probably don't) indicate prostate cancer. The thought that keeps going through my mind today is that I hope I'll be OK. Is that the correct use of the word hope? Absolutely, 100% yes! It is a belief in a better future and there's loads I can do to take action and hopefully confirm that it isn't prostate cancer but – in the unlikely event that it is – there is loads more action that I can take. That's hope.

Hope is a choice

I'm not going to pretend that life is always easy but as you've already seen in this opening chapter, hope makes things better. It can be a self-fulfilling prophecy if we believe that things will be better and then do everything in our power to make it so.

Things are better when we choose hope. Hope is a strategy.

3

A brief history of hope

Pandora's box – hope is all that remains

Hope had a really mixed press in Ancient Greece! It was seen as a source of comfort, but also as a possible source of deception linked to suffering. In Hesiod's 'Works and Days',[10] we read of Pandora (the first mortal woman) who was beautiful and charming but also very curious. She was given a jar (often translated as a box) by Zeus and warned not to open it. The box contained all the evils of the world such as death, poverty, and disease.

Despite the warnings, curiosity got the better of Pandora and she opened the box and released all the evils into the world. Realizing what she had done, she quickly closed the lid but it was already too late and the evils were now in the world. Although not everything flew out of the box. Just one thing remained. Hope.

---

[10] www.perseus.tufts.edu/hopper/text?doc=Perseus%3Atext%3A19 99.01.0132%3Acard%3D1

There are many interpretations of this story, with Pandora's box often being used as a metaphor for something that is best left untouched because we never know what might come out.

I see a really positive interpretation here; sometimes when life is incredibly difficult and there are lots of challenging things going on in the moment, hope is all that remains. We need to get through things and get to a better place. But even though hope is there, it might still be hidden in the box and we need to seek it out. We need to unleash hope. We need to choose to find hope.

Christianity – hope is a firm assurance

Thomas Aquinas stated that hope is: 'A future good, difficult but possible to attain… by means of the Divine Assistance… on Whose help it leans'[11] which really sets the scene for hope being focused on a promise for the future, but with the assurance of God making that a reality.

Hope sits alongside faith and love as the three key Christian virtues and the Bible often refers to the firm assurance of hope, for example, 'Surely there is a future and your hope will not be cut off',[12] 'For

---

[11] https://en.wikipedia.org/wiki/Summa_Theologica
[12] Proverbs 23:18 (ESV)

I know the plans I have for you, declares the Lord, plans for welfare and not for evil, to give you a future and a hope'.[13]

However, hope isn't just future-focused in the Bible and there are many references to the role that hope plays in helping people survive suffering. The book of Romans[14] talks of how people rejoice in the hope of God and that people know that suffering produces endurance, endurance produces character, and character produces hope.

So, in Christianity, hope is a firm assurance of a better future, along with a recognition that there might be challenges along the way.

Islam – hope balanced with fear

In Islam, hope (*raja*) is based on a firm belief in Allah and is differentiated from passive or wishful thinking (*tammani*). It provides an absolute assurance to believers. I find the distinction between hope and wishful thinking helpful, and it is often illustrated by how a farmer would plant crops, water, and tend to them and hope for results. So, hope isn't just about staring at the ground and wishing things would grow, it is about putting in the work and

---

[13] Jeremiah 29:11 (ESV)
[14] Romans 5:2–5 (ESV)

hoping. In Islam, hope is often talked about as a source of comfort and resilience during challenging times, encouraging people to be optimistic even in the most difficult of times as things will get easier.

Hope (*raja*) sits alongside fear (*khawf*), often described as being like two wings of a bird where both are needed. Too much hope on its own can lead to complacency whilst too much fear on its own can lead to despair.

Hinduism – hope comes with frustrations

The concept of hope in Hinduism is complex and nuanced;[15] hope involves longing for specific outcomes which brings optimism. Whilst hope can build resilience in the longer term, it can initially lead to despair and frustration. Hope serves as a source of encouragement to help people navigate life's challenges.

Hope is inextricably connected to belief in a higher power but whilst hope can help people endure suffering, true happiness is said to come from transcending hope and achieving contentment.

---

[15] www.wisdomlib.org/concept/hope

Buddhism – wise hope

Buddhism draws a distinction between different types of hope.[16] Ordinary or 'unskilled' hope is based on a craving for what we think we want and can lead to a cycle of attachment and disappointment and despair. In contrast, wise hope involves seeing things as they are, being realistic and practical about what we hope for, and 'lightly holding' hope for the benefit of all beings, with hope and fear being two sides of the same coin.

The Enlightenment – the birth of secular hope

For centuries, hope was predominantly a religious concept, intertwined with faith and divine intervention. However, the Enlightenment, spanning from the seventeenth to the nineteenth centuries, marked a pivotal shift. During this era, hope began to transcend its religious roots, evolving into a secular force that emphasized human potential and agency. Enlightenment thinkers championed the idea that logic, reason, and science could solve problems and drive progress across various domains. This new perspective on hope inspired societal reforms,

---

[16] www.lionsroar.com/ask-the-teachers-what-is-the-buddhist-view-of-hope/

particularly in law and individual rights, as people began to believe in their capacity to shape their own futures.

Influential figures like John Locke and Montesquieu were at the forefront of this movement, advocating for justice and inspiring hope-driven revolutions aimed at societal change. This secularization of hope shifted the focus from divine intervention to human agency, emphasizing tangible improvements in the present world rather than solely in the afterlife. While religion continued to play a significant role, hope was increasingly grounded in the potential for real-world progress.

However, not all Enlightenment thinkers embraced this newfound secular hope without reservation. Voltaire, through his work 'Candide'[17] critiqued excessive reliance on hope, warning against a lack of critical engagement with reality. Despite such criticisms, the Enlightenment solidified hope as a forward-looking belief in humanity's ability to make meaningful progress and improve the world.

The Enlightenment's legacy of secular hope continues to influence modern thought, reminding us of the power of human agency and the potential

---

[17] Voltaire, F.-M. A. (2011). *Candide*. Gardners Books. (Original work published 1759.)

for positive change. As we navigate the complexities of today's world, this era serves as a testament to the enduring belief in our capacity to create a better future through hope.

The modern era – hope is as vital as ever

Whilst technological and medical advances have put us in a better position than ever, it can also be argued that things are more uncertain and volatile than ever, a situation that requires us to be hopeful.

When we view hope through the lens of our capability to make things better, we have much to be hopeful for. The amount of progress we have made, and knowledge created, across science, medicine, technology, and AI is massive. This is really well demonstrated by the Existential Hope platform[18] which, through their website, podcast, Hope Drop Newsletter, and XHope Library aim to encourage people to look at the future through a positive lens and focus on what is possible. This encouragement to explore new innovations and how we can use them to drive positive change in the world typifies hope in the modern era. It can also be argued that social media has in many ways, democratized hope, as it

---

[18] www.existentialhope.com/

opens up communication channels and amplifies voices that may not otherwise be widely heard.

Whilst hope has often been viewed as an individual characteristic, it is interesting to view the power of hope in social movements. Activists such as Martin Luther King Jr, unite people around hope for a better future. His 'I have a dream' speech[19] is a story of hope. He speaks of a momentous decree 100 years earlier that 'came as a great beacon light of hope' but had still not been fulfilled, talked of his refusal to believe that it was not possible, and encouraged people not to 'wallow in the valley of despair'. The speech then continues with the parts that are still well known today:

'I have a dream that…

I have a dream that…

I have a dream that…

I have a dream that…

I have a dream that…

This is our hope.'

In many ways, the speech is a masterclass in how leaders can inspire hope. Whilst not wallowing

---

[19] www.npr.org/2010/01/18/122701268/i-have-a-dream-speech-in-its-entirety

in the despair, the challenges are called out and acknowledged before moving on to paint a vivid glowing picture of a better future, and encouraging people to take the necessary action to make it so. That's hope.

The recent Covid pandemic is still fresh in our minds. Many of us sailed through it relatively unscathed and were fortunate, but some people lost their lives, or lost loved ones, or had really challenging times through illness and isolation. In fact, many people are still struggling with the impact today. Even though it was challenging, hope kept us going. That strong belief that it wouldn't always be like that and it would get better again.

Even though they're not calling it hope, Generation Z seem to be reclaiming hope, but naming it 'locking in'. For a group that are sometimes accused of being the most distracted of all, unable to focus on anything for very long, locking in has become a trend. The term appears to have originated in sporting culture but has now spread into common usage. To lock in on something is to lock in on a goal or an outcome and to do what it takes to get there, making any necessary sacrifices along the way. I don't mind what we call it, I'm just delighted to see hope in action.

Even though we live in volatile and uncertain times, we can argue that we have more reason than ever to be hopeful.

Academic research on hope

Hope research has – over about three decades – focused on the importance of hope in helping people to thrive, and has typically focused on the elements of people having positive expectations for the future, identifying what they can do to make that a reality, and having the ability to navigate the 'bumps in the road' along the journey.

Modern 'Hope Theory' is partly rooted in Charles Snyder's research into excuses (cited in Eliott, 2005);[20] in lab experiments, Snyder and others sought to understand more about why and how people make excuses for not achieving outcomes. This deep dive into the science of excuses led Snyder to explore the opposite of making excuses (although it isn't quite that simple), which led to the development of Hope Theory. So, hope is the opposite of making excuses. Sort of. Snyder views hope as a cognitive (or thinking) process comprising agency thinking (the motivation to achieve goals) and pathway

---

[20] Eliott, J. (2005). *Interdisciplinary Perspectives on Hope*. Nova Science Publishers.

thinking (the ability to identify routes to achieve those goals). Snyder's research was foundational as it showed that hope was measurable, that it could be developed (rather than being a fixed characteristic), and that it could improve the achievement of goals, our resilience, and our mental health.

Shane Lopez built upon Snyder's research and developed it further,[21] defining hope as the belief that the future will be better than the present alongside the conviction that we have the power to shape that future. His expanded view of hope was that it comprised: (1) goals thinking (setting attainable goals); (2) pathways thinking (strategizing to achieve goals); and (3) agency thinking (the motivation and energy to pursue goals). Lopez showed just how much of a difference hope could make, particularly exploring how this impacted academic success. High hope students did well academically, got good grades, and had low levels of anxiety. In contrast, low hope students struggled, had lower confidence, and were significantly negatively impacted by any setbacks. I'm a big fan of Shane Lopez's whole body of work but two things in particular stand out for me: (1) that hope is teachable; and (2) that hope is contagious. As

---

[21] Lopez, S. J. (2013). *Making Hope Happen: Create the future you want for yourself and others*. Atria Books.

we'll explore throughout this book, hope isn't some mythical random state, rather it is something that can be achieved and developed through deliberate practice. And I love the contagious nature of hope; that our hope can be a spark to others and can ignite a flame.

When I see organizations which are negative and struggling with toxic behaviours, I feel a bit frustrated as there is a whole field of academic research on Positive Organizational Scholarship and Positive Organizational Behaviour that has lots of learning that would help. Fred Luthans has contributed heavily to the field of Positive Organizational Behaviour through his work on Psychological Capital (PsyCap). Psychological Capital comprises four components – hope, efficacy, resilience, and optimism – and has been found to enhance workplace performance and wellbeing as well as contributing to leadership effectiveness and having positive societal impacts. Luthans draws heavily on Snyder's hope theory and has made a great contribution to the field of hope research by showing how practical hope interventions have a positive impact in increasing hope. In the work of Lopez and Luthans (as well as many others) is it clear that hope is teachable. Hope is learnable. That is great news as it means that we can indeed choose hope.

In the earlier research, the emphasis has been on hope as an individualistic characteristic with interventions aimed at increasing personal hope. Subsequent research by Allan Bernardo challenged this individualistic approach, even suggesting that a bias in the wording of the questions in the Dispositional Hope Scale encouraged the elements of hope to be seen as individualistic. Bernardo went on to propose the concept of locus-of-hope, suggesting that hope was not entirely individual and that external factors (family, peers, and spiritual beliefs) might play a part.

More recently, Rachel Colla's work[22] has taken our understanding of hope to a whole new level. Colla has criticized existing approaches as too linear and individualistic and has proposed taking a dynamic systems view of hope. In particular, her research methods around participatory narrative inquiry have furthered a deeper understanding of hope. In particular, Colla's work extends current thinking beyond the will-power and way-power and also adds the why-power (meaning and purpose) and the who-power (the relationships with people that sustain and encourage us).

---

[22] https://pmc.ncbi.nlm.nih.gov/articles/PMC8906075/

I'm fascinated by the fact that hope can be a game for more than one player and I'm always keen to understand more about the leadership and people aspects of hope. My own research 'Is hope a strategy? A thematic analysis of individual experiences of hope within teams' (undertaken as part of my MSc Applied Positive Psychology and Coaching Psychology at the University of East London) has sought to dive deep (using qualitative analysis) to understand people's stories and help inform what leaders can do to help people find hope. We'll return to the findings of my research in Part 3 of this book.

Part 2

Building hope

4

When hope goes wrong

Hope is often seen as a beacon of light, a guiding star that leads us through the darkest times. But what happens when hope goes wrong? When it becomes a trap rather than a lifeline? I want to explore some of the less-discussed aspects of hope – those that can lead us astray or leave us stuck.

Learned helplessness: the invisible cage

Imagine being in a situation where you know you can escape, but suddenly, the walls close in, and no matter how hard you try, there's no way out. This is the essence of learned helplessness, a concept brought to light by Martin Seligman's research.[23] There's lots I don't like about the research which entailed giving mild electric shocks to dogs, but the

---

[23] Seligman, M. E. P., & Maier, S. F. (1967). Failure to escape traumatic shock. *Journal of Experimental Psychology*, 74, 1–9.

findings are powerful. Dogs were put into a cage with two sections, one of which had a mat at the bottom which would give them a mild electric shock. Some of the dogs could easily jump to the other side of the cage to avoid this, which they soon did. However, the other dogs were in cages which had a divider inserted so they couldn't jump to the other side and had no choice but to endure the discomfort. After this, dogs were all mixed together and were put into cages without a divider, so it was very simple to move to the other side and avoid the discomfort. Many dogs did that immediately but half of them didn't; the dogs who had been 'conditioned' to believe that there was no escape from the discomfort simply lay down and endured it, even though it only required a simple act to escape from it. The barriers still existed in their minds, even though they were no longer actually there. I dislike the experiment, but refer to it often. We can become conditioned to believe that our efforts are futile, even when the barriers are no longer there. This state of learned helplessness (or hopelessness) is dangerous. It strips away our sense of agency, leaving us feeling trapped in a cage of our own making. It's easy to judge those who seem unwilling to help themselves, but often, the barriers they face are invisible to us. Recognizing and addressing these mental barriers is essential to breaking free from this cycle.

Toxic positivity: when optimism turns sour

In a world that often champions positivity, it's easy to fall into the trap of toxic positivity. This is the belief that we must always maintain a positive outlook, regardless of the circumstances. However, this can erode genuine hope. By ignoring real concerns and pretending everything is fine, we risk losing touch with reality. True hope is not about blind optimism. It's about acknowledging challenges and working through them. Overdoing positivity can lead to disappointment and disillusionment, ultimately destroying the very hope we seek to cultivate.

Manifesting versus hope: the action gap

Manifesting has gained popularity as a way to achieve our dreams, but it's often misunderstood. Many believe that simply visualizing their goals will make them a reality. However, without action, manifesting remains a dream or a wish. True hope involves taking steps towards our goals. It's about making informed decisions and taking small, consistent actions. While envisioning our desires is important, it must be coupled with effort to transform hope into reality. Whilst very popular, there is evidence that manifesting does not work. Whenever anybody shares their experience with me of it working, they talk about the manifesting (being clear about what they want and maybe creating a vision board) but then they also talk about making different decisions and taking action. That is more than manifesting. That's hope.

The danger of false hope

Is hope ever a bad thing? The debate continues, but one thing is clear: false hope can lead to devastating let-downs. In medical training, clinicians are taught to avoid giving false hope. They provide realistic outcomes and possibilities, allowing patients to hold onto hope while understanding the reality of their situation. Hope should exist within the realm of realistic options. It empowers people to strive for the best possible outcomes without setting them up for disappointment. Even in the face of terminal illness, people can still be really hopeful, but hope can be redirected towards achievable goals, such as leaving a legacy or ensuring a peaceful end. False hope is damaging. Hope is about playing the cards we've been dealt. Please don't get me wrong as I'm not suggesting that hope should always be practical and unambitious. Hope can be audacious and involve shooting for the moon, but – in those situations – we need to be really careful about how we deal with 'failure', something that we'll return to in Chapter 9.

Avoiding naive optimism

Naive optimism is the belief that everything will work out without any effort or consideration of potential obstacles. This mindset can be self-destructive, leading to complacency and inaction. Hope should be grounded in reality, encouraging us to take proactive steps towards our goals. By acknowledging the challenges, we face and preparing for them, we can maintain a hopeful outlook without falling into the trap of naive optimism.

5

Finding hope

In Chapter 4, we explored lots of possible reasons why we can lose hope and reasons why we might get stuck. We're now going to look at what we can do about that. I've already said that hope is teachable, and hope is learnable. We can view hope as a repeatable process.

Hope isn't about naive optimism, or wishful thinking, or false hope. Rather hope is a very realistic, energizing, and motivating state. Shane Lopez[24] defines Hope in terms of Goals, Agency, and Pathways, in other words knowing the future state we want, feeling that we have agency to achieve it, and knowing how to get there (including navigating obstacles). Hope involves showing up and working on the right things. One of the consistent themes in the Hope research is that in order to have hope,

---

[24] Lopez, S. J. (2013). *Making Hope Happen: Create the future you want for yourself and others.* Atria Books.

people need to be able 'to see how they can get there from here'. If they can't see (or believe) it, then hope isn't fully there.

Dr Hanna Kampman (Programme Director of UEL's MSc Applied Positive Psychology and Coaching Psychology) always says that re-search is me-search – in other words the self-reflection – is a vital part of research. In an early piece of work on hope, I was doing some journalling and self-reflection and realized that even though I had a really nice life and always scored highly for Hope and Positivity in strengths assessments, I felt like I had very little hope at the time. I felt really overwhelmed and almost as if I didn't even 'dare to dream' as I didn't feel hopeful about making these things a reality. It was a really frustrating place to be as I also got some emotional contamination and the feeling of hopelessness spread to a few other situations. And once you lose hope, you become a passenger. So, I had a big incentive for my work on hope and my me-search and research led to me creating the 'Hope Playsheet'. I designed this so that we could try to mechanize hope, to make it a repeatable process, and to put it on autopilot when we need it. I deliberately called it a Playsheet rather than worksheet as I know that the mindset of playing and experimenting can evoke less pressure than when we feel like it is work!

You can download a copy of the Hope Playsheet at https://hope.tips/hope-playsheet where you will also find other helpful resources relating to hope.

Figure 2 illustrates the Playsheet, and we'll explore each element in turn.

Hope	What are you hoping for?
	Strengths to use:
Options and **O**bstacles	Consider alternative ways to achieve what you're hoping for. What might get in the way?
	Strengths to use:
Plan	Create a clear plan so that you 'can see how to get there from here'
	Strengths to use:
Engage	How will you show up, engage with the plan, and navigate obstacles?
	Strengths to use:

Figure 2 Hope Playsheet

I deliberately found a way to make this an acronym for HOPE as I wanted to make it really simple and easy to remember. Here are the stages:

1 Hope

We start with what you're hoping for. Hope is an active thing and always has an object. Hope is specific and we hope 'for' something, so we need to know what this is. I'm a big fan of Gallup's CliftonStrengths™ and use strengths as part of my work. I've deliberately provided space for people to reflect on which of their strengths they'll use to help them answer that section as when you know you can be resourceful and use your strengths to answer something, you can be confident that you can do it. To answer what you're hoping for might sound obvious, and often is, but it is sometimes missing. Sometimes we don't allow ourselves time and space to dream, to lift up our eyes and think about how we want things to be. Sometimes we feel like we daren't even dream. Sometimes we're so overwhelmed by a situation that whilst we can articulate what we definitely don't want, we might not be able to easily describe what we do.

You might be able to answer this section really easily or it might be something that you want to ponder on, or take your time to think about and keep adding to as inspiration strikes. In an ideal world, what you're hoping for should excite you when you read it. It is also important to note that it might also scare us at the same time. That can happen because of the dissonance between where we are and where we want to be, or because we feel overwhelmed (or worried about) the steps to get there. That needs to be put to one side for now and we can just focus on what we're hoping for, and how we want things to be.

2 Options and Obstacles

This is where we start to prepare for action, for making the hope a reality, and by considering alternative ways to achieve what we're hoping for and considering what might get in the way. One of the keys to success in this stage is not to overthink things as we get to evaluate them in the next stage. Just because we write down an action or a blocker, it doesn't mean that we're committed to it, it is just that we will give it some consideration in the next stage.

For Options, I encourage people to brainstorm and just think about all the things they need to (or could) do to make the hope a reality. This works really well with a load of sticky notes, an online brainstorming or outlining app, or I sometimes use an app to dictate ideas so that I can let my brain run free. You don't have to worry about the order you're going to do things in or whether that's the optimal way to get there, you just need to identify all the things you need to (or could) do. This is very similar to one of the stages in David Allen's Natural Planning Model (NPM) approach[25] where brainstorming actions is part of defining and initiating a project. Hopefully you start to feel excited at this stage, but, if you find yourself worrying, rest assured that you'll have the opportunity to do that in a considered way shortly. For now, just let it flow! You might also find that you start to identify totally different paths to get to the destination and that's great, just remember that you don't have to evaluate them and make any choices quite yet.

Obstacles can be really interesting and is the section where you might need to watch your mindset. It might feel negative, but it isn't. You're considering these things now so that you can increase hope and raise the chances of success. We'll return to this in more detail when we look at the leadership aspects of hope but, for now, take the same brainstorming approach as you did for Options. Think about all the things that could go wrong or be barriers to stop you getting what you hope for. Many of the obstacles will be external and might relate to other people.

[25] Allen, D. (2015). *Getting Things Done: The art of stress-free productivity*. Piatkus Books.

I'm always surprised how many obstacles I identify that relate to one person: me! Using knowledge of how we succeed at things and what trips us up can provide huge insight that helps us build hope. We can learn so much from previous challenges and use the learning to build hope.

3 Plan

This step can sometimes take a while to complete but is still very worthwhile. This is where we get to make sense of all the things we need to do to achieve what we're hoping for. We get to sequence the actions, maybe put them into phases, and sometimes create several pathways for how to achieve what we're hoping for. We also get to review the obstacles and start to think about how we'll avoid them, or deal with them if they occur. Once we've got the plan, it should really give us a feeling that we can see how to get there from here, still recognizing that we might feel some dissonance because of the gap.

4 Engage

This is where the magic starts to happen as this is where we get to figure out how we will show up, engage with the plan, and navigate the obstacles. The first three sections of the Hope Playsheet prepare us for this section as this is where we show up, do stuff, and move towards what we're hoping for. Again, your knowledge of how you succeed (and why you don't when you don't) will really help you to improve this section to increase your likelihood of success.

I'll share two personal examples that I've addressed using this section. In any fitness or health journey one of the things I know about myself (from lots of previous experience!) is that my thinking can be very polarized, it can be very black and white. For example, I am either an endurance athlete or an inactive lazy person. I don't do shades of grey in between, I'm either one or the other in my mind. I anticipate this as an obstacle as it can trip me up. For example, I frequently have a few days without exercise as I'm traveling for work and I know I'm going to be hectic with limited time. Even after this, I might have a few hectic catch-up days or even catch a cold and be unwell for a few days. So, I might end up with ten days without exercise, which feels like a big deal for somebody who typically does at least six to ten hours of cycling workouts each week. The thing I know about myself is that ten days without exercise can lead me to then think that circumstances don't (and will never!) allow me to be an endurance athlete and so I might as well give up. Which I do. Knowing this about myself lets me: (a) deliberately practice some self-compassion in those circumstances; and (b) have a 'get back on the bike' protocol with some regular easy go-to workouts that let me, literally, get back on the bike. It is very simple, but leaning into what seems like the negative side of hope and anticipating the challenges has been a game changer in my life. Second, I know I can be a terrible procrastinator and, through previous experience, I can most likely predict the things I'm going to procrastinate on. Knowing that lets me anticipate it and prepare for it. Sometimes I break things down into smaller chunks when I know I'm likely to feel overwhelmed, other times I might introduce some accountability and arrange to do something in partnership with someone. All of this learning and self-knowledge increases hope.

I use the Hope Playsheet frequently for both myself and with coaching clients. In the interests of openness, I'm sharing a completed example I created a little while ago to help me prepare for my Everesting cycling challenge. At the stage I completed this Playsheet, I was only a few weeks post-surgery, I'd managed one minute of cycling and I'd burst into tears after getting off the bike (with my crutches propped against the bike) because I was so pleased I could turn the pedals. After a few weeks of managing a few more minutes on the bike, the thought of a cycling challenge that is – for me – similar to running four marathons back-to-back in one day was overwhelming. The Hope Playsheet helped me make significant progress, as shown in Figure 3.

I will now share some helpful 'hope' techniques.

| **H**ope | What are you hoping for? |
| | Strengths to use: Futuristic, belief |

To complete a successful Everesting challenge.

This will be a huge achievement, especially after breaking my ankle. To use it to raise money for (and awareness of) Hope for Justice, and I know that this will change lives for people trapped in modern slavery and victims of human trafficking. I will be really grateful to have recovered to the point where I can do this, and will have reached a fitness level that I've not had for years.

Not only will I learn more about training, cycling, and fuelling for a big challenge but I'll learn a lot about myself as well.

| **O**ptions and **O**bstacles | Consider alternative ways to achieve what you're hoping for. What might get in the way? |
| | Strengths to use: Strategic, self-assurance |

Load of things I'd originally typed as a hope are actually options that I'd self-imposed as goals: To complete it: (1) this year; (2) in a good time; and (3) as an official (i.e. < 1 day) challenge. None of these are mandatory and all are optional. I'll use the TrainerRoad training plan set to attempt it in six months.

External obstacles: I don't know how well my ankle will recover and to what extent and I can never know this in advance so my previous approach of set a big goal, commit to it publicly, and work hard towards no longer fits. I need to work at it and listen to my body.

Internal obstacles: in response to a huge goal that is getting closer, I know that I might progressively feel increasingly overwhelmed to the point where I give up. I also know that if I feel bad about the challenge in some way, then I might simply avoid it.

| **P**lan | Create a clear plan so that you 'can see how to get there from here' |
| | Strengths to use: Strategic |

Week 1 – keep it really simple and small and do 3x30-minute 'Tick Tock' route on Zwift. The aim is simply to be back on the bike and learn how my ankle will hold up.

Week 2 onwards – based on how my fitness is progressing and my ankle is feeling, create a training plan for the following week in response to what I've learned.

Immediately: I feel bad as I haven't told people that my original plan is impossible so I will update people about my new plan (that has no date and no self-imposed constraints!).

Ongoing: make sure I keep checking in on my hope and share this with others as a way of communicating the bigger picture and my progress

| **E**ngage | How will you show up, engage with the plan, and navigate obstacles? |
| | Strengths to use: Focus, relator, learner |

First three rides are now booked in my diary. Before each ride, remind myself of what I'm really hoping for and think about my learning after each ride. Find an accountability buddy to check in with. Use Strava to check in and – most importantly – be grateful for whatever I've managed to do.

Figure 3 Example Hope Playsheet

1 Never ever lose hope

As we saw in the opening chapters, despair and hopelessness are not good places to be and where we lose a feeling of hope in some areas, that can spread and reduce the feeling of hope in others. We'll cover some techniques below and how we can sustain hope but if you're pursuing what becomes an impossible goal, or the cost of pursuing that goal is a price you are no longer willing to pay, then we'll explore some ways to exit gracefully. Ideally, take action to build your hope every day, even if only by a little bit. If you lose hope, you give up your agency and you become a passenger of whatever is happening. If you're losing hope, pause and reflect what the obstacle is that is causing that feeling, figure out what you can do around it and then do a hope reset and get moving again.

2 Build your cheerleading squad

Some challenges are not a game for one player; when we hope for something big, the journey can be challenging. Finding your squad, your cheerleaders, your tribe, can be vital. Lots of people may not be interested or care about what you are striving for but there will be people who get it, get you, and want you to succeed. It might be in person or it might be online, but I'd encourage you to find your tribe of people who can encourage you in the pursuit of what you're hoping for, and you can encourage them. My own way of doing this is to have people with whom I have an occasional 'strategic latte'. I've talked about strategic lattes for years, and they are simply the process of sitting down with somebody I know and trust, enjoying a nice coffee, and spending time openly talking about them and how they're doing and about me and how I'm doing. I always find strategic lattes to be really powerful as they help me to take a beat, and pause for a moment. They often help me reflect on how much progress I've made, and they always help me see things from a different perspective.

3 Measure the right things

When we set off on a journey to pursue something we're hoping for, it can take a while and we need to be intentional about how we view success. It is all too easy to always see the gap to where we want to be, and we need to find some way of seeing how far we've come. That said, the measures that spring to mind may not always be the most helpful ones. For my Everesting cycling changes I have some measures such as my FTP (Functional Threshold Power) which I re-measure every month that gives me a sense of progress but I am conscious that this is very much an outcome goal, a consequence of doing all the training. And outcome goals lag behind the progress and can fluctuate. As anyone who has been on a diet can tell you, the scales don't always reflect the victories and they can fluctuate despite you heading in the right direction. Outcome goals are powerful but they are often best paired with process goals (for example, this week I did six hours of cycling) so we can feel pleased for putting the effort in, even if that isn't yet leading to the outcome. Whatever you pick, you need to find a way to pause and celebrate the progress you're making, making sure that you don't just attribute things to luck (remembering the difference between fortunate and lucky).

4 Borrow hope where you need to

If we're falling a little short on hope then other people can jump-start our hope and we can borrow hope from other people. I've done this on my Everesting cycling challenge as I'm not a natural endurance athlete. When starting my training, my hope needed a bit of a jump-start and I'd watched films and video of people sharing their Everesting journeys and watched somebody live stream their actual challenge. They gave me a bit of a jump-start to get me going. I often need inspiration on the bike as it can be a long hard slog for hours. With indoor cycling (on a smart trainer) I can watch something on TV at the same time and I've often borrowed hope by watching the Tour de France and Tour de France Femme avec Zwift as I ride. That helps!

5 Do a hope reset when needed

Sometimes when things feel frustrating and you feel like you're losing hope, I'd encourage you to go back to your Hope Playsheet. Revisit what you've written. Maybe write it again from scratch. Rather than just keep going if things don't feel like they're working, hitting reset, switching things off and back on again can get you back on the right track. Oftentimes, a hope reset just involved finding a different path to the same place, but a path that you didn't maybe identify at the start.

6 Don't be afraid to scale down

Sometimes we set off in pursuit of something we're hoping for but it turns out we've made it bigger and more challenging than it needs to be or we actually want it to be. Don't be afraid to scale back your ambition and either recognize that this will be phase one and you'll do the other phases after this, or maybe this is phase one and you'll decide what else to do when you get to the end of this phase.

7 Never give up hope, but feel free to drop something you were hoping for

Don't abandon hope, but do feel free to abandon what you were originally hoping for. If you've tried the techniques to achieve it, and to get support, and you just don't want to do it any longer or it simply isn't worth the personal cost then that's not abandoning hope, that's a sensible decision. Make a decision not to pursue that, and reflect on what you've learned. As we keep coming back to, the learning is valuable and will help you on other hope journeys. I know that – in the past – when I've abandoned hope on something, that feeling has 'leaked' into other areas of my life and affected me. Now, I might choose to drop an outcome or scale it down, but I'll do it with self-compassion. There's a world of difference between abandoning 'a' hope and abandoning hope.

8 Keep your eyes on the prize

Even though we set off in pursuit of something we're hoping for, we can easily get distracted by things that don't matter. Some things matter, most don't. I could pick thousands of work examples of me being distracted by things that don't matter, but I'll start with a cycling one. I often do long endurance cycling rides on Zwift, a virtual cycling platform that recreates the feeling of cycling and lets me ride lots of routes with other cyclists from around the world. I might be doing a few hours of zone 2 riding where I'm doing a gentle ride and I won't even get out of breath. That's what takes me towards the thing I'm hoping for. Then a group of people will overtake me and I'll speed up and join the peloton, I'll take my turn at the front and then drop back into the group and enjoy the benefits of drafting behind the leader before regularly taking my turn at the front. And there's a real sense of camaraderie and we might exchange a few messages on the platform. And then I'll remember what I'm supposed to be doing and that I wasn't supposed to be a sweaty mess so I'll drop back and run (well, cycle) my own race. And then a few minutes later, I see timing lights across the road and Zwift displays my PB (personal best) time for that sprint section over the last 90 days and I'm tempted to sprint rather than do what I'm there to do. As a recovering people pleaser, I know that I can fall into the trap of getting distracted and wanting people to like me more so than I do want to achieve the outcome. There are all sorts of distractions, we just need to keep our eyes firmly fixed on the prize. Even though it isn't a universal truth, from my days of competing in dressage (at a very low, local level) I learned that where I look, I go. I learned to be careful about my focus. This is where things such as a 'vision board' can be helpful, where you construct a board that makes the vision a reality and put it somewhere where you will see it every day. It simply helps to keep our eyes on the prize.

9 Beware misguided perfectionism

Perfectionism sometimes gets really mixed reviews, so let's be clear about it; in some situations, perfectionism is absolutely necessary and a really good thing. For instance, if I'm undergoing surgery then I want my surgeon to be a perfectionist. I really want them to focus on getting things right. There are many similar situations where perfectionism is a great thing. However, what can get in the way of hope is where we apply perfectionism when it isn't needed or helpful, something that we term 'misguided perfectionism'. Misguided perfectionism has lots of negative consequences and can be a major source of procrastination. For example, when an author stares at a blank page and worries about crafting the perfect book chapter, they can freeze. The solution? Lower the stakes. Write for the bin, accepting that the scrappy first draft won't be great but is the first small step on the road to something that is.

10 Don't procrastinate

I know a lot about procrastination. Partly through my studies and research, but mostly through having many years of experience of being really good at procrastinating. Procrastination destroys hope. Procrastination is where we spend time not doing something, or worrying about something, or finding activities that make us feel like we're doing something without actually doing it, and procrastination can be incredibly wasteful emotionally. Procrastination destroys hope because it stops us taking action that moves us towards the destination, towards that outcome that we want.

Also, procrastination often entails repeatedly worry-ing about something, whether that is worrying about actually doing it, or worrying about the conse-quences, or worrying and catastrophizing about it going wrong, or even finding something else quite innovative to worry about. I really like what David Allen[26] says about these thoughts, pointing out that the only reason to have a thought on more than one occasion is if you enjoy having it. In other words, if it is a really happy thought then feel free to enjoy that as often as you want, but if you're worrying

---

[26] Allen, D. (2003). *Getting Things Done: The art of stress-free productivity*. Penguin.

about something, then you just need to have a plan for dealing with it so you can put it to bed and forget about it.

Whether you want to journal to get to the heart of why you're procrastinating, or simply use a little hack to help you work around it, it is worth addressing as procrastination diminishes hope. Your solution might involve breaking things into smaller chunks, making sure to 'eat the frog' and do the most difficult thing at the start of the day, or to use the Pomodoro technique and set a timer for 25 minutes during which you will only focus on the task in hand. Regardless, procrastination is worth addressing.

11 Comparison can be the thief of joy

Social media can be an amazing tool to broaden your network and bring us all closer together but – depending on how we use it – can also hinder hope. I've been taking selfies so that I can track my fitness journey and I follow a lot of fitness influencers so I regularly see them sharing before and after photos of either themselves or their coaching clients. Looking at those doesn't tend to make me hopeful because even my after photos look like the before pictures for many of their clients! We can get stuck in doom scrolling on social media and comparing our journey with others. One of the great things about social media is that we can curate our feed, and it is worth thinking about what you want to see that will build your hope.

From insights (on finding hope) to hope

Summary of key points

Hope isn't fixed. It is teachable and learnable. It is about having a vision for the future, knowing how to get there, taking the steps to get there, and navigating the bumps in the road along the way.

The Hope Playsheet:

Hope	What are you hoping for?
Options and Obstacles	Consider alternative ways to achieve what you're hoping for, and anticipate what might get in the way.

Plan	Create a plan so you 'can see how to get there from here'.
Engage	How will you show up, engage with the plan, and navigate obstacles?

Helpful hope techniques:

1 Never ever lose hope – hope is precious, always hold onto it.
2 Build your cheerleading squad – surround yourself with people who sustain your hope.
3 Measure the right things – get some early indicators that increase your hope.
4 Borrow hope where you need to – if you're running low on hope, borrow some.
5 Do a hope reset when needed – if you're totally stuck, hit reset and go back to the Hope Playsheet.
6 Don't be afraid to scale down – if what you're hoping for is overwhelming you, just scale it back. For now.

7 Never give up hope, but feel free to drop something you were hoping for – just make sure you come out of it with learning that increases your future hope.

8 Keep your eyes on the prize – there are so many distractions, keep focused on what you're hoping for.

9 Beware misguided perfectionism – only be perfect when it is absolutely necessary.

10 Stop procrastinating – either address the root cause or use some hacks to get moving.

11 Comparison is the thief of joy – especially on social media. Curate your feeds so that they build hope.

Your key reflections

What has made you think? What do you want to think about more deeply? Where are your opportunities?

Turning key reflections into hope

- For anything you want to address, how do you hope it will be in the future?
- What are your options, all the ways that you could get there? What are the obstacles?
- Now, what's your plan?
- How are you going to keep showing up and engaging with the plan?

Part 3

Hopeful leadership

6

An introduction to hopeful leadership

Leaders need to bring hope

In Chapter 2, we explored Gallup's research on what people want from leaders, exploring how people want hope, trust, compassion, and stability. However, hope was the primary need, far outweighing all the others and ranking significantly higher than the second ranked need, trust. Hope gives people something to look forward to and helps them to navigate challenges whilst working towards a brighter future. Gallup found that where leaders provided hope, it increased thriving and reduced suffering and that hope was the leading need across all types of leaders (including education, organizational, political, religious, and family). Finally, the need for hope was mentioned more by younger people (aged 18–29 years) possibly reflecting the fact that people have their whole lives ahead of them and really value hope.

Napoleon Bonaparte is credited with saying 'A leader is a dealer in hope' and I agree that helping their teams and organizations be hopeful is a vital part of a leader's role. I believe that leaders need to maintain their own hope, help each person in their team find, sustain, and build hope and do the same for the team as a collective.

Is hope a strategy? The key findings from my research

Having briefly introduced my own research in Chapter 3, I'm going to explore the key findings as well as lots of other additional observations. We'll dive deeper to each of these in turn, but Figure 4 shows an overview of the key themes that emerged – it is a thematic analysis of individual experiences of hope within teams.

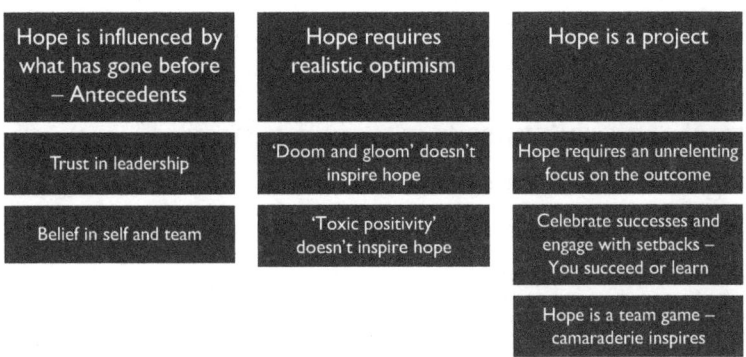

Figure 4 Research themes overview

7

The ghosts of past hope

I've called this chapter 'the ghosts of past hope' because when you try to build hope in others, there are things that have gone on before, the antecedents, that will influence the way people hear you and whether they believe you. These antecedents may be as a result of things you've done, things your predecessors have done, or other things that people have experienced. Regardless of where they have come from, they are real and we need to be aware of the ghosts of past hope. Not only does this help us understand how people may hear and view what we say as leaders, it serves as a useful reminder that things we do today will set the foundation for people to be hopeful in the future.

Trust in leadership (and you as a leader)

If you are going to stand up as a leader and paint a picture of a future vision, there is normally no guarantee that you will get there. As people listen to you, a huge part of them deciding whether to feel hopeful about that future is the extent to which they trust you as a leader. I believe that in interpersonal relationships of any kind, trust is one of the most valuable commodities we have. Every interaction, everything you say, everything you do (or don't) will either build or diminish trust.

Virtually every article or research paper that I've ever read, all quote the same Dutch proverb; 'Trust arrives on foot, but leaves on horseback'. In other words, trust takes a long time to earn – sometimes years – but can be lost incredibly quickly.

It doesn't matter what you say when you're trying to build hope, if you've destroyed trust in the past why should anyone believe you now?

Let's take two bad examples that I've witnessed throughout my career:

1 **The restructure:** These are probably my least favourite change initiative as I've witnessed them dozens of times and I am not a fan. Typically, a new leader will come in and will want to improve things quickly and make their mark. So often, there are loads of opportunities to improve things in organizations so this sounds like a very attractive promise if you take it at face value. Typically, you'll design a new organization

structure or 'target operating model' in which you slightly change some of the reporting lines and boxes on the organizational chart. You'll then follow a really structured process to see who maps to their jobs and then give other people notice that they're 'at risk'. What follows can be a lengthy process where people apply for these jobs (often their own jobs). Even though leaders will often reinforce the importance of 'keeping the lights on during the change', there is usually an inevitable hit to productivity and services. We're human after all and it is hard to give something your all if you're feeling let down, or worried about the future, or worried about how you're going to pay the mortgage. Eventually, the restructure is complete, and you'll stand up and declare it a great success. The organization may not be functioning any better, you've unsettled people, there's some 'survivor guilt' in those people who 'survived' the process, people are struggling with change fatigue if this is a regular occurrence and have learned to care less as a survival technique, you've lost a lot of really good people who left as they could easily find employment elsewhere, and you've spent quite a bit of money on redundancy payments and compromise agreements. But hey, you've said it is a great success so that's all good! I know I sound really negative about this but I've witnessed it countless times and heard hundreds of stories of this. If you are a leader who leads initiatives that create the illusion of hope and result in a lot of effort to keep things the same (or even make them worse) then this will cost you in the future; the ghosts of past hope will catch up with you and you'll inevitably find that you're trying to fill people with hope and you'll be left wondering why they don't get it.

2 **Spin:** I'll keep it deliberately anonymous, but I remember a change of a very senior leader in an organization. The previous leader was widely respected, was well known and visible across the organization, and would make their email address known when speaking at events so it was easy to get in touch with them and they would always respond. However, it is fair to say that their face didn't fit in the light of some wider restructuring (see above!) and they were managed out and a new person (whose face definitely did fit) arrived. Not wanting to be bothered by lots of people getting in touch with them, an additional email address was set up for the office of this person and huge announcements were made

about how – for the first time ever in history – it was possible to communicate with the very important person in this role. Apart from, it wasn't. In the past, you could email the very important person in this role and receive a reply. Now, you could email a shared account managed by the comms team and receive a reply from one of the comms team, purporting to be from the leader. Again, if you do one thing and claim it to be something else then don't get surprised if the ghost of past hope bites you on the bum!

My research findings

In my own research, trust was identified as a fundamental pillar of hope by all participants. Where people trusted their leaders, they felt hopeful when faced with a challenge and sustained that hope throughout the journey.

Some leaders clearly stood out as a beacon of hope, with one participant saying 'there were a couple of key people in that who gave us hope. Probably the main one being the chairman at the time, who was a very sort of just positive character and you thought well, if anybody can get something sorted out, he can'. In addition to hope in individual leaders, some participants highlighted leadership teams as providing hope, with some noting that increasingly diverse leadership teams and seeing more women in leadership roles gave them hope.

Specifically, trust in leaders was commonly mentioned as a key factor in hope; one participant stated that 'Trust is a foundational element in relationships; that significantly impacts hope and motivation' whilst another highlighted that hope could be significantly affected by one person, noting 'Hope diminished because my relationship and trust with [senior leader] diminished'. Where trust diminished, so did hope.

Whilst this trust was sometimes personal or relational, several participants talked about trust in the wider organization or system, as opposed to individuals. One commented 'When individuals feel that the system does not advocate for or care for them, it creates a desperate situation that undermines hope' also commenting on the difficulty of having hope of things getting better 'when you've been in a very large sort of system for some time and something has gone on for a long time, it's very difficult to trust the system or the institution'. Where an organization proves over time that things won't improve, it is difficult to ask people to suddenly have hope. Where a system was described as hopeless, it is a big ask to expect people to suddenly have hope.

Transparency and honesty were consistently described as vital in maintaining hope. One spoke of intentionally leaning into difficult situations and saying 'We just have to be really honest with [you]… and say we're really sorry, but we can't' rather than avoiding or delaying the conversations. This transparency builds trust which, in turn, enables hope. Whilst leaders often had a tendency to try to avoid bad news, many participants talked about the power of sharing bad news, one saying 'If I've got the bad news, I can get on with it' as opposed to dealing with the uncertainty of not knowing. Transparency appears to have a positive cascading effect whilst a lack of transparency appears to have the opposite effect. One participant spoke of the importance of transparency in all situations, but especially when there has been a change of direction or a failure noting the consequences of a lack of transparency; 'the grumblings start. I think you lose respect, you know, within the organization and that can then move to a loss of engagement which then can move to a loss of productivity…' further commenting that 'what can happen if you're not transparent is just loss of trust… and then that has a lot of different ramifications because then people will start to lose faith or lose belief or lose hope'. Whilst honesty was a common theme, one participant drew a distinction between genuine and non-genuine honesty, asserting that 'Genuine honesty increases hope, because you can see through non-genuine'. It looks like you can't fake honesty, at least in the longer term.

How leaders behaved during periods of organizational change was a recurring theme and one participant spoke at length of the need for leaders to maintain trust during significant organizational change. The importance of treating people well was emphasized, both for employees who left and who remained in the organization, noting 'If you've got an employer that makes you feel that you're trying to do your best for people... it makes people feel more hopeful about the future'. Constant organizational change caused a problem for some people, particularly where this was a 'restructure', changing the organizational reporting lines, resulting in some redundancies. Where this was the case, one noted 'You introduce a change every couple of years, the other one hasn't landed', something that is problematic for the organization where people are promised the hope that a reorganization will make things better but – before that better future is seen – another restructure is announced, again promising a better future.

Unfortunately, some participants joined an organization filled with hope but that quickly diminished when they realized there was a difference between what they had been promised and the reality on the ground. One participant stated 'I definitely stepped into it with hope' but added 'My hope diminished the longer I saw how things were being done'. In this regard, hope appears to be fragile and can easily be broken, something that was experienced by several participants. Where something was promised as genuine but turned out to be a tick-box exercise it, unsurprisingly, diminished hope.

Rachel Botsman's work on trust

If you're going to provide hope as a leader, then building and maintaining trust is vital. I whole-heartedly buy into Professor Rachel Botsman's assertion[27] that 'Money is the currency of transactions, but trust is the currency of interactions'. Botsman builds upon earlier research and presents the four traits of trust in a compelling way, focusing on 'how you do things' (competence and reliability), and 'why you do things' (integrity and empathy). If we explore the earlier research by Dietz and Hartog[28] then it provides some further insight into how

---

[27] www.nbforum.com/nbreport/rachel-botsman-economy-trust/ #:~:text=%E2%80%9CMost%20businesses%20that%20we%20 interact,is%20now%20more%20of%20it

[28] www.researchgate.net/publication/237845587_Measuring_ Trust_Inside_Organizations

we can build trust as a leader. I've mapped this to Botsman's presentation of the research to show the alternative names for the traits.

The foundational pillars of trust

How you do things

- **Competence/Ability** describes perceptions of leadership competence in doing their job or fulfilling their role.

- **Reliability/Predictability** emphasizes how leadership behaviour has to be consistent or regular over time.

Why you do things

- **Integrity** defines how trustworthiness is linked to being seen as someone who adheres to principles of fairness and honesty while avoiding hypocrisy.

- **Empathy/Benevolence** describes a concern for others beyond leaders' own needs and showing levels of care and compassion.

If you want to provide hope, you need to build the foundation of trust and it is worthwhile reflecting on these traits and remembering that people will assign you a level of trust based on what you say, what you don't say, what you do, what you don't do, what you choose to tolerate and many other things beside. If you want to provide hope, first you must build trust.

Belief in self and team

It was clear from my research that as people listen to you share a hopeful vision of the future, they'll listen to what you say and form a judgement on whether it can be delivered. There are lots of considerations about you as a leader and the organizational culture, but a lot of it comes down to the person themselves and the team they're part of. And it boils down to one thing; have we got confidence in that person and the team to deliver. As a leader you need to be focused on developing each and every member of the team so they can be their best and feel confident, as well as making sure you build high-performing teams.

In Gallup's research on Team Effectiveness, 70% of the variation in team performance (from the off-the-scale amazing down to the dysfunctional) was explained by one factor; the manager. Management and leadership development is vital if we are to help build hope. It is also clear that teams are where the magic should happen and this coming together of different strengths should help teams to truly be greater than the sum of the parts. Yet, this often doesn't happen and so many teams are either dysfunctional or, at least, not performing as they could be. In my work on helping organizations build hope, team performance is a common barrier. My go-to tools for improving team effectiveness are Patrick Lencioni's book[29] if the challenge doesn't appear too difficult, and Richard Hackman's book[30] if it appears that it needs a much deeper dive to help the team.

My research findings

Past experiences figured highly with one participant speaking of having hope in a new role, 'I guess there's a good chunk of experience in there. You know, I'd had a very similar experience in a previous job where everybody told me, that I spoke to, that it was completely chaotic and, you know, I was able to bring some order and some sort of common sense to it'. These past experiences could sometimes result in a person feeling hopeful whilst others around them felt hopeless, with one elaborating 'The situation for the business felt hopeless. But me personally I found that situation quite invigorating'. There was

[29] Lencioni, P. M. (2011). *The Five Dysfunctions of a Team*. John Wiley & Sons.

[30] Hackman, J. R. (2002). *Leading Teams: Setting the Stage for Great Performances*. Harvard Business School Press.

a real sense of 'success breeds success' where people would bring that confidence and self-assurance from past situations, resulting in them being hopeful.

The successes predicating self-assurance weren't always easy. Several participants had seen significant success following periods in their lives where they had really struggled as a result of things such as death by suicide of someone close to them, workplace bullying, or post traumatic stress disorder (PTSD). In these cases where someone was now thriving, the past experience gave them hope when they, other people, or the organization faced challenges. Many of the journeys of hope had been difficult, with one sharing a story of success 'after two years of absolute horror', and these successes inspired future hope.

Where the participants had a high degree of control – and didn't need to depend on anyone else for the outcome – that seemed to be associated with feeling hopeful, and the same was true where participants had a high degree of influence on the outcome. One stated 'I was relatively hopeful and I probably would say I, I thought 50 to 75 percent of it was in my influence', concluding 'I genuinely believe there's always something in my gift'. Their attitude reminded me of the first of Steven Covey's habits[31] about being

[31] www.franklincovey.com/courses/the-7-habits/habit-1/

proactive, about focusing on the things we can influence and letting go of the rest. Of controlling the controllables and accepting the things that we can't change. Covey's work has sometimes been criticized as coming from a position of privilege and whilst I agree that we need to be mindful of that, I also know that I personally have probably wasted months of time getting frustrated about things that – ultimately – I can't do anything about.

Perceived team effectiveness was also mentioned by most participants in deciding how hopeful they felt, with one describing several aspects of this in their team, commenting on passion for a common purpose, 'Drawing on other people's energy, other people who have a passion or an energy for a cause, for a purpose, for ideally a common purpose. Certainly that reinforces hope very strongly, I think, with other people', of being inspired by people in the team 'when people inspire you, when you see things that people do we got onto that sort of that belief that mankind will be all right because this person has just done this wonderful thing and that fills me with hope', and the impact of the wider team 'but we did have the wider team… and their belief that… they were on the journey as well'.

Trusting colleagues in the team was mentioned by several participants with one commenting 'So

I think at the moment I'm surrounded by a lot of people who I feel you can trust, and that makes me hopeful'. Another spoke of the importance of faith in team members, pondering how this was vital to hope, 'If I've lost faith, have I also lost hope?'. Similarly, one participant expanded on the elements of hopeful team relationships, noting 'I think it's finding people that you trust. Finding support. Finding loyalty. Recognising competence in people. That's very reassuring'.

The power of complementary teams was mentioned by several participants, with one stating 'The way that I build those teams is to find those individuals that are complementary to each other, but not the same'. Complementary strengths and weaknesses was mentioned – 'I went in with a degree of excitement and a genuine belief that it was doable… It really helps to have people who understand you, care about you, know your weaknesses as well as your strengths'.

Leadership style also influenced the degree of hope people felt, with one speaking of the negative impact of micromanagement, 'I find micromanaging stifling' and another sharing how they had previously been that type of manager 'I used to be the kind of manager that really struggled… I was micromanaging, I was stifling people from learning' but had learned and now realized not to do that to the team as 'every time they make a mistake, they learn something and I really do sit back now I see the value in doing that'.

Where a team had access to coaching and development, that increased hope. One participant talked about using 'a coaching approach' to help other people find hope, encouraging them to 'try and look at the pros and cons' and 'think about the impacts… of what it is that they are trying to achieve'. Similarly, another talked about coaching as a tool, noting that they helped people find hope 'through coaching conversations, I would say, a real good look at the current reality, a real good look at where do we want to be, and then some analysis on the steps to get from one to the other'. Coaching didn't only increase hope in the participants, it could also increase hope with the person doing the coaching; when one participant was asked what increased their own hope, they responded 'Coaching, doing my coaching really gives me hope because I see the value of it with the [staff] that I'm working with'. Another commented on the important of staff development, commenting 'having like investment and staff and to actually skill people up, I think is really important' and when describing their own experience of being developed, 'That gave me a lot of hope because I felt invested in'.

I want to reflect on the role of coaching as it touches on a key point. I don't believe that you can really give hope to people, but you can help people to find it. There are some exceptions (surgery would be one example) but most examples people share of giving hope to others is more focused on helping the other people to jump-start hope, giving them a nudge in the right direction. *When Helping Hurts*[32] is a book that stopped me in my tracks when I first read it. Aimed at churches and other organizations doing outreach and development work, it explores how well-intentioned initiatives can hurt by creating a dependency, plastering over the root causes, and possibly inducing a sense of shame. When we wade into a situation we don't understand (especially in a different context or different country), we might misunderstand what is going on, take a materialistic view of the solutions, and inadvertently disempower those we're seeking to help by adopting a bit of a 'God complex' where we see ourselves as the saviour and fixer. All of these things are the opposite to what we actually want to happen. Please, in any situation remember to take an asset-based approach and help people use their resources and capabilities. Jump-start hope where necessary, but the focus should be on helping people to find and build their hope. Coaching is one way of doing this

---

[32] Corbett, S., & Fikkert, B. (2014). *When Helping Hurts: How to alleviate poverty without hurting the poor... and yourself.* Moody Publishers.

and I don't mean that you have to have a professional certified coach for every situation, even through that is helpful in some. Rather, I believe that all managers and leaders need some level of basic coaching skills so that they can truly empower other people and help them find hope. In this context, The Hope Playsheet can be a powerful coaching tool as you can gently guide someone to think through the steps.

From insights (on the ghosts of past hope) to hope

Summary of key points

Hope is heavily influenced by what has gone before. That might be either good or bad news depending on how you or your predecessors have behaved. Regardless, the great news is that you can take actions today that build hope in the future.

Trust is a foundation of hope.

1 Trust is a precious commodity that takes time to earn, but can be lost in the blink of an eye.
2 Some leaders are beacons of hope. Ideally, be one. If not, find people who are and amplify their voice.

3 Remember that every interaction with people either builds or diminishes trust and, therefore, either builds or diminishes hope.

4 Lead an organization that people can trust.

5 Transparency and honesty are a vital component of hope. If you hide things, it diminishes hope.

6 Organizational change can be challenging and isn't always the right answer. If you need to do it, don't keep plodding through the steps of constant restructures and expect people to have hope.

7 Don't promise something to people to build hope if you know you can't deliver on it.

Self-belief (both personally and for the team) is a foundation of hope.

1 Past experiences of success build hope. Recognize, celebrate, and remember them.

2 Surviving difficult challenges builds hope. These stories are powerful.

3 Control the controllables. Know the difference between what you can control or influence and what you have to accept. Focus on what you can do.

4 Team effectiveness is vital. Build diverse teams of capable people, with complementary strengths and help them work well together.

5 Don't micromanage people.

6 Provide coaching and development. It increases hope.

Your key reflections

What has made you think? What do you want to think about more deeply? Where are your opportunities?

Turning key reflections into hope

- For anything you want to address, how do you hope it will be in the future?

- What are your options, all the ways that you could get there? What are the obstacles?
- Now, what's your plan?
- How are you going to keep showing up and engaging with the plan?

8

Realistic optimism

The title of this book mentions 'why realistic optimism is essential for effective leadership' and finding this middle ground between 'doom and gloom' and 'toxic positivity' is a crucial balance that we will now explore.

Doom and gloom doesn't inspire hope

I think this is pretty obvious but if we want to inspire hope in people, we can't exclusively focus on doom and gloom. Even though I think this is obvious, there is a lot of doom and gloom about and you'll find plenty of this in politicians and other leaders. I suspect that some of this might be a result of a (misguided) desire to build 'a burning platform' to convince people of the need to change. Obvious I know, but listing all the problems we have doesn't necessarily leave people feeling hopeful, excited, and inspired for the future.

I listen to a lot of podcasts and one of the political podcasts in the UK would always feature (the now former) Prime Minister Boris Johnson saying 'The doubters, the doomsters, the gloomsters – they are going to get it wrong again' so I've heard him saying that hundreds of times. We'll return to Boris Johnson in the next chapter on toxic positivity, but I can see that he was sharing a message that people wanted to hear. If all we see and hear are problems, then we lose hope. Leaders can't spend all their time spreading worry about the future.

In a world where negativity often dominates the narrative, it's easy to feel trapped in a cycle of despair. Doom and gloom, with a relentless focus on problems and catastrophes, can leave us feeling stuck, hopeless, and disengaged. But why does this happen, and how can we break free from this paralyzing grip?

The trap of overwhelming negativity

One of the primary reasons doom and gloom fail to inspire hope is their ability to keep us stuck. The constant barrage of negative news and predictions of worsening conditions can be overwhelming. This focus on catastrophe, both present and future, can lead to a state of apathy. We become frozen, unable to act or even imagine a way forward.

Disempowerment

Another critical factor is the lack of empowerment that comes with a doom-and-gloom mindset. When we concentrate solely on the negative, we often overlook the actions we can take to improve the situation. This leaves us feeling powerless. Without a clear path forward, we are not motivated to act, and the cycle of inaction continues.

The power of hope and optimism

In contrast, focusing on solutions and possibilities can inspire and empower us. Hope serves as a counterbalance to negativity, providing a vision of a better future. When we believe that our actions can lead to progress and improvement, we are motivated to take steps toward that brighter future. Optimism fuels this motivation, encouraging us to act and move toward positive change.

Breaking free from despair

To break free from the paralyzing effect of doom and gloom, we must shift our focus. By emphasizing solutions and the potential for improvement, we can inspire hope and empower ourselves to act. We need to choose to embrace optimism and hope to envision a future where our actions make a difference.

In a world filled with challenges, it's crucial to remember that hope is a powerful force. By choosing to focus on solutions and possibilities, we can break free from the grip of doom and gloom and move toward a brighter, more hopeful future.

In a book about hope, why do I feel the need to focus so much on doom and gloom? There's an easy answer; because there is so much of it about. There are loads of reasons for this, as I outline next.

1 Bad is stronger than good

According to Baumeister:[33]

'The greater power of bad events over good ones is found in everyday events, major life events (e.g., trauma), close relationship outcomes, social network patterns, interpersonal interactions, and learning processes. Bad emotions, bad parents, and bad feedback have more impact than good ones, and bad information is processed more thoroughly than good. The self is more motivated to avoid bad self-definitions than to pursue good ones. Bad impressions and bad stereotypes are

---

[33] Baumeister, R. F., Bratslavsky, E., Finkenauer, C., & Vohs, K. D. (2001). Bad is stronger than good. *Review of General Psychology*, 5(4), 323–370.

quicker to form and more resistant to disconfirmation than good ones. Various explanations such as diagnosticity and salience help explain some findings, but the greater power of bad events is still found when such variables are controlled. Hardly any exceptions (indicating greater power of good) can be found. Taken together, these findings suggest that bad is stronger than good, as a general principle across a broad range of psychological phenomena'.

We easily get caught up in the 'the deficit discourse' where we only talk about the bad and ignore the good. One personal example comes from my regular travel between Manchester and London using the train. It isn't that uncommon for the train to be late or for the train to be overcrowded. What happens on these days is that we end up starting conversations with other passengers on the train about how bad it is and we'll all be on social media sharing messages about the experience. What happens on days when everything is great and the trains run perfectly on time? Nothing. Silence. My experience of that train journey is mostly positive, but you might not deduce that from my social media posts. That's the danger of the deficit discourse; if we only notice and share what's bad, we no longer even notice what's good.

2 We remember the bad stuff

I really like Rick Hanson's comments[34] on this; 'The brain is like velcro for negative experiences, but Teflon for positive ones'. If we're biased to notice the bad stuff and more likely to recall it, no wonder we can get stuck in doom and gloom if we have a bias to noticing and then remembering the bad stuff!

3 The field of psychology hasn't helped enough

It could be argued that rather than change this approach, the fields of psychology has reinforced and encouraged it. According to Linley (quoted in Tunariu & Boniwell, 2019),[35] that was not actually the plan:

> 'Unbeknown to the general psychology population, there were three tasks of psychology prior to World War Two (WWII). These were to: a) cure mental illness; b) enhance the lives of the normal population; and c) study geniuses. Due to the aftermath of two world wars and the return of many

---

[34] Hanson, R. (2020). *Resilient: How to grow an unshakable core of calm, strength, and happiness.* Harmony Crown.

[35] Tunariu, A. D., & Boniwell, I. (2019). *Positive Psychology: Theory, research and applications.* McGraw-Hill Education.

psychologically impaired soldiers, research funding focused on its first agenda, with the other two nearly forgotten'.

4 Well-intentioned alternatives can make things worse

Positive psychology is a relatively new field of psychology, and with evidence-based disciplines lagging behind, it could be argued that many people have filled the void by creating alternative approaches which are based on positive thinking. Indeed, a brief search on social media – especially Instagram – will quickly highlight lots of accounts encouraging positive thinking with messages such as 'you are enough', 'you've got this', 'you are loved', or encouraging people to 'manifest' their future desires so that the Universe can provide. These approaches aren't rooted in evidence, and some can – in fact – be counter-productive.

My research findings

Participants talked about lots of 'positive' and 'negative' things in describing hope, sharing nuanced perspectives and sharing stories of hopelessness as well as hope.

By definition, hope requires a positive vision for the future. One participant described hope as 'being optimistic about the future, it's having something positive to hold on to, to keep in mind', and another drew the distinction between situations where 'I felt really quite hopeful' and 'I wasn't particularly hopeful'. Where negativity was prevalent, that was associated with despair and loss of hope. Many participants spoke of the need to actively engage with and channel the negativity, with one saying that 'you can create hope... by ensuring that you're not allowing a situation to develop where despair or negativity is unnecessarily created' and another similarly focusing on the need for a positive focus, 'for me, hope is tied into the belief that things will always work out, that things will get better eventually even if you go through some stuff that isn't great. I think it is tied in with optimism, and I'm not always positive, but I believe there will be a positive outcome'. Most participants drew a distinction between needing to engage with (and not ignore) the negatives to be hopeful, but always focusing on a positive (or better) outcome. For example, one described hope as 'an acknowledgement, of what isn't going great and a real push towards improving that, positive movement' and another spoke of the need for realism, saying 'I always have a vision and a picture of where I want to be and I hope we can get there, but it has to have some realism attached to it'.

Not only did participants talk about the need for a positive outcome to have hope, but many also talked about the ability to find hope, even in seemingly hopeless situations. One shared that 'Even in the most hopeless of situations, there's something that I can hold on to'. Participants shared details of really traumatic experiences, but were able to still find hope. One spoke of how 'Even in dark situations, I think and I believe, I'm generally a hopeful person'. Several participants shared situations where hope was focused on the best possible outcome within their control in a situation where no outcome was that great. For instance, one worked in a context involving end-of-life care, sharing 'We did amazingly good deaths, which sounds bizarre, but we did it really, really well'. Even in end-of-life care, there was hope.

Many participants shared experiences of hopelessness or of hitting rock-bottom. This was a difficult place to be, with one reflecting 'That feeling that I've been talking about throughout our discussion, that was beginning to eat away at me and that's just not a good place to be in really'. Many participants talked about the effect of losing hope in one domain, and how those feelings could spread, with one saying 'I think if you're in a negative space then you're not going to have any hope that anything can be any different'. However, where somebody arrived fresh into a seemingly-hopeless situation, there seemed to be a benefit associated with being 'the new person', with one participant sharing 'Hope for me straight away is I'm new into this role and actually it's easier sometimes, isn't it? When something's at rock bottom you come in and you can find easy wins and you can improve things'.

There are so many reasons why we might get caught up in a bit of doom and gloom but it doesn't inspire hope in other people. Instead, we need to focus on a positive vision for the future. Just not excessively positive. That brings us neatly onto the subject of toxic positivity.

Toxic positivity doesn't inspire hope

In a world that often champions the power of a positive mindset, it's easy to overlook the potential pitfalls of overdoing it. While positivity is undeniably a healthy and beneficial approach to life, there's a fine line beyond which it tips over into being toxic. This phenomenon, known as toxic positivity, occurs when the insistence on maintaining a positive outlook becomes excessive and inauthentic. It dismisses genuine emotions, pressures individuals to remain upbeat regardless of circumstances, and discourages open discussions about challenges.

Positive emotions are important, but there's loads of reasons not to overdo it. Barbara Held[36] raised concerns about the consequences of the 'tyranny of the positive attitude':

'The tyranny of the positive attitude lies in its adding insult to injury: If people feel bad about life's many difficulties and they cannot manage to transcend their pain no matter how hard they try (to learn optimism), they could end up feeling even worse; they could feel guilty or defective for not having the right (positive) attitude, in addition to whatever was ailing them in the first place. This is a possible unintended consequence of trumpeting positivity, whether in popular or professional circles. For according to the wisdom of our popular culture, what ails one in the first place might have been avoided, or at least ameliorated, with positive thoughts. This popular message is certainly reinforced by extensive research findings that reliably demonstrate that optimism and positivity are linked to health and longevity, whereas pessimism and negativity have the opposite effect.'

---

[36] Held, B. S. (2004). The negative side of positive psychology. *Journal of Humanistic Psychology*, 44(1), 9–46. https://doi.org/10.1177/0022167803259645

Positivity is good. Excessive positivity is bad! There are several reasons why toxic positivity is damaging and why we need to find the right balance:

- **Suppressing negative emotions:** One of the most glaring characteristics of toxic positivity is its tendency to suppress negative emotions. In environments where this mindset prevails, expressing feelings of sadness, worry, or fear is often discouraged. Phrases like 'look on the bright side' or 'stay positive' become mantras, leaving little room for acknowledging genuine emotions. This suppression can lead to a culture where negative emotions are seen as undesirable, pushing individuals to hide their true feelings.

- **Promoting unrealistic optimism:** Toxic positivity also fosters an environment of unrealistic optimism. The belief that everything will always turn out brilliantly, even when evidence suggests otherwise, can be damaging. This mindset not only sets people up for disappointment but also erodes trust. When reality doesn't align with overly optimistic expectations, it can lead to feelings of betrayal and disillusionment.

- **Invalidating genuine feelings:** Another detrimental aspect of toxic positivity is its tendency to invalidate people's feelings. In toxic environments, experiencing negative emotions can be perceived as a failure or a sign of weakness. This can lead to feelings of guilt or shame for simply experiencing normal human emotions. The pressure to conform to a relentlessly positive outlook can make individuals feel isolated and misunderstood.

- **The dangers of suppression:** The dangers of toxic positivity extend beyond emotional suppression. When negative emotions are consistently brushed aside, it can lead to burnout and mental exhaustion. Moreover, avoiding engagement with difficult problems means that critical issues are often ignored, leading to unresolved conflicts and strained relationships. The inability to address and process genuine emotions can significantly damage personal and professional relationships.

In my experience, toxic positivity results in problems on two main levels, as discussed below.

1 Promising unicorns and rainbows

Toxic positivity often results in overselling the outcome. I've seen it in politics loads of times, where things have been incredibly difficult for years and then politicians promise that it is going to very quickly transform to being amazing. I promised that

I'd return to the subject of Boris Johnson, and he was many times accused of 'Boosterism',[37] the deliberate act of inflating something or deliberately talking it up. If you can deliver unicorns and rainbows then that's great, but otherwise promising them is going to: (1) disengage people as they won't believe you in the first place and might do a sneaky eye roll as they listen to you; and/or (2) their trust in you will be diminished when we don't reach the promised land and you'll find it difficult to inspire hope in them in the future.

2 Diminishing the challenges

The other classic element of toxic positivity is to diminish the challenges and pretend that things will be easy. I'm sure that this is often well-intentioned in a desire to keep people hopeful, but it is misguided. Presented with a hopeful view of the future, some people (me included) will naturally focus on the positive and will pay attention to all the reasons why it will be OK. Others will find a list of reasons why it won't work. As somebody who has a natural inclination to lean towards toxic positivity, I don't mind confessing that I can find people who immediately list all the reasons it won't work to be

---

[37] www.independent.co.uk/voices/boris-johnson-jeremy-hunt-speech-brexit-b2270634.html

deeply annoying. And valuable, because they are the people I need around me. As a leader, if you are seeking to inspire hope in people for a better future there will be some people who can intuitively anticipate the barriers to achieving that better future. And you need to listen to them and – in fact – go much further and encourage them to speak.

Listening to – and being seen to deal with – concerns actually inspires hope because it increases the likelihood of achieving the better future.

Psychological safety

We can learn a lot from Amy Edmondson's work on psychological safety.[38] In her study of teamwork in hospitals, she set out to prove that high-performing teams made fewer errors but was surprised by the initial research findings that suggested exactly the opposite! Teams who reported effective teamwork experienced more errors. She had a hunch as to why that might be so and started to examine the data in more detail and conduct further research. Her hunch was correct and the conclusion was that better teams were more willing to report mistakes because they felt safe to do so.

---

[38] Edmondson, A. C. (2018). *The Fearless Organization: Creating psychological safety in the workplace for learning, innovation, and growth.* John Wiley & Sons, Inc.

Let's explore some definitions from Edmondson's work; Psychological safety is 'a shared belief that the team is safe for interpersonal risk-taking'. It involves an environment where individuals feel comfortable expressing themselves, sharing ideas, asking questions, and admitting mistakes without fear of negative consequences such as humiliation, punishment, or rejection. This concept emphasizes the importance of creating a climate where team members feel respected and valued, allowing them to contribute fully and engage in open and honest communication.

It is clear to see how a climate of high psychological safety can increase hope as there are benefits on many levels; Psychological safety leads to team members feeling more engaged and motivated, because they feel that their contributions matter and that they're able to speak up without fear of retribution. It can lead to better decision-making, as people feel more comfortable voicing their opinions and concerns, which often leads to a more diverse range of perspectives being heard and considered. Finally, it can foster a culture of continuous learning and improvement, as team members feel comfortable sharing their mistakes and learning from them.

Amy Edmondson defines four levels of psychologically safe team dynamics and I believe all four are necessary to build hope in teams and organizations:

1 **Learner safety:** Team members should feel comfortable asking questions, experimenting, learning from each other's mistakes, and looking for new opportunities.

2 **Collaborator safety:** Team members should participate in open dialogue, have mutual access to each other, and engage in constructive debates.

3 **Challenger safety:** People should feel comfortable challenging the status quo if they identify changes that need to be made, even if those changes are unpopular or difficult. Team members should be encouraged to speak up and expose problems.

4 **Inclusion safety:** Team members need to feel valued. Everyone should know that their experience and ideas matter equally, regardless of their title or rank. Members should be comfortable contributing to the group.

I'd recommend engaging with Amy Edmondson's work directly, but there's just one last component that I want to explore here; the behaviours of psychologically safe leaders. There are three that, in my view, particularly reinforce hope:

1 **Set the stage and acknowledge own mistakes and concerns:** To put if bluntly, if we

expect other people to be honest, admit mistakes, and be open about what worries them, how can we expect them to do it if we won't do it ourselves. I know I have to keep this in my mind at all times as I'll sometimes get inadvertently caught up in the view that we need to show 'strong' leadership and not show any weakness or express doubts or concerns. We know that's not true; people need to have confidence in us and trust us when we promise a better future but vulnerability aids that, not hinders. We need to always be mindful of role-modelling the behaviours we want to see from our teams.

2 **Frame work as learning:** We'll come back to this as a separate topic but turning challenges into an opportunity to learn (and always be learning) can be a game-changer for some people. More on this soon.

3 **Model curiosity:** It is so easy to be judgemental about other people and to engage in mind-reading about why they behave the way they do or get concerned about particular things. However, being judgemental tends to lead us into a closed mindset. If we make up our minds about somebody, confirmation bias can kick in and we stop fully listening. We can stop

listening fully, only hearing what confirms our view of that person. If that happens, we miss out on so many opportunities to build hope. Curiosity (another form of learning!) can be such a helpful tool to help us keep an open mind; I wonder why they're concerned about this project? I wonder why they're so worried about that particular thing? Curiosity can help us really understand what is going on, and – as leaders – we set the scene for others.

My research findings

Where leaders engaged in toxic positivity by being overly positive and over-promising as well as ignoring or dismissing legitimate concerns, this did not inspire hope in the long term. One reflected on their past experiences of hope with leadership, noting, 'It wasn't there with [them], that was probably blind optimism' sharing a story of how a hopeful vision was agreed, but then that was not evident in further actions. More hope than was warranted was promised, which was followed by a slump in hope. Another expanded on the damaging effects of overdoing hope, saying 'people often go into an environment full of hope... and that can bring them to a state of hopelessness'.

Several participants shared situations where leaders had engaged in toxic positivity and created false hope by leaving people with the expectation that something would happen, that was – in reality – never going to happen. One shared an example where 'Short term it gave people false hope because they thought that instead of reporting into [A], they'd be reporting directly into [B]' and there were many examples of toxic positivity and false hope providing a short-term boost in hope, followed by a slump. Another shared an example of constant organizational restructures, and their lack of belief in the vision that was being promised, saying 'the "hope" is that this will be okay, but there's nothing, there's no substance to say that it's going to be okay' and 'But then, also, what I see is false hope coming from leaders that we're getting rid of [x] people and replacing them with junior members of staff or no members of staff, and everything will be fine'. Where leaders described a positive future that the participants did not believe, hope diminished.

Whilst many of the stories focused on the impact of toxic positivity at the start of a journey, some participants shared stories of the impact of toxic positivity during the journey. One talked about a situation where leaders were sharing lots of good news stories, and simply ignoring the challenges.

They described their experience, 'I understand that celebration of success. We all need to be geed along by that, but it feels a bit like gaslighting... amidst some of these really serious things that are going wrong'. They further explained that hope wasn't about just focusing on the positive for them, rather:

> 'But that isn't what hope is for me. Hope is an acknowledgement, of what isn't going great and a real push towards improving that. Positive movement. That's, for me, where hope lives. It almost lives in the despair place, not in a brainwashing or a gaslighting place, there's a real authenticity that comes with hope. To be hopeful, we need to first acknowledge where we are, don't we?'

Participants has a similar response when there was a serious issue that leaders claimed to have solved, but the response was perceived as a superficial 'sticking plaster' or diminishing the real issues, with participants describing leaders' response as 'pathetic'. For instance, one described a situation where there is a sense of both organizational and individual collapse, and that this was being addressed by a wellness week involving 'free croissants and a hand massage'. Where participants perceived a response as tokenistic, it damaged hope with one saying:

'it just makes me want to swear, you know,
how is that going to do anything for what is
going on both to structures and to the internal
well-being of your staff, it's just. Excuse me,
********! It's just ******** and I can't bear
it, you know? But it feels part of the whole
system now that we're sticking plasters over
with a free croissant.'

If you want to explore more on toxic positivity,
I have found Susan David's work[39] to be incredibly
helpful. David focuses on the 'tyranny of positivity'
and how that is damaging as it results in emotional
suppression, encourages inauthenticity in relationships, and denies reality. Instead, David argues for
emotional agility which doesn't force us to choose
between positivity and negativity, but encourages us
to embrace emotional wholeness. In my experience,
this is a really powerful approach.

Compassionate truth

I want to return to the topic of why some things
that need to be said don't get said. Many years ago,
I was observing a leadership team for a few hours
before I worked with them, and I sat quietly in the
corner paying attention to what was and was not

---

[39] David, S. (2018). *Emotional Agility*. Penguin.

being said, being especially interested in what was being avoided. Based on that experience, I drafted a model of compassionate truth as shown in Figure 5.

My hypothesis was that people either spoke the truth, avoided it, or sometimes lied and they did this with either negative or positive intent. I was a bit judgemental of what I was seeing, which is reflected in the initial labels I used but it did seem to fit with what I was seeing. Time and time again, I would see avoidance (which I initially termed cowardice which was unfairly judgemental) and people would avoid saying something that needed to be said. Until their frustration built up to the point that they couldn't take it any longer and it all came out in one blurted out stream of feedback which might be perceived as rudeness as it was coming from a place of frustration.

Speaking truth	Rudeness	Feedback
Avoiding truth	Ambivalence	Avoidance
Speaking lies	Nastiness	White lies
	Negative intent	Positive intent/ compassionate

Figure 5 Compassionate truth

They were still speaking the truth, they just weren't doing it from a good place. The solution that I have seen work thousands of times is to encourage people to lean into being open to give and receive feedback as a regular everyday occurrence. That way, it can be simply speaking the truth with positive intent.

Helping people to give and receive feedback well is – in my experience – often one of the quick wins in building hope as it is simple to teach and often has a big positive impact.

My go-to approaches are to encourage people to use a really simple model for giving feedback:

- Situation: rather than be vague and say 'you always do that', be very specific about a situation.
- Behaviour observed: say what you saw. The other person might see it differently, but that's fine and it is important that you share your perspective.
- Impact: talk about why this matters and, possibly, the impact of not addressing it.
- Invite input: have a conversation about it.
- Agree action: reach agreement on what you're both going to do in response to the feedback.

Note that this is most definitely not 'the feedback sandwich' that comes across as insincere and doesn't really allow for discussion. Rather, this is an open two-way discussion. And please don't fall into the trap of thinking that feedback is always about 'catching people doing things wrong' – don't forget the power of catching people doing things right! And when we give 'positive' feedback, we want to make sure that we're being every bit as specific as when we're providing 'negative' feedback.

Giving quality feedback is only part of the job though, and we need to make sure that we all receive feedback well. That can be difficult for some people as some of us, me included, can occasionally take feedback as criticism that cuts straight through to our soul! I've developed a really simple model to help people receive feedback well. Please note that I sketched this out on a slide late one night a couple of years ago and I think I created it and didn't read it elsewhere! I've searched high and low and can't find any reference to it anywhere.

How to receive feedback well: CARE

C **Clarify:** Before reacting, make sure you fully understand the feedback. Ask questions to clarify anything that seems unclear or vague. This shows you're engaged and willing to listen.

A Acknowledge: Acknowledge the feedback without defensiveness. Show appreciation for the other person's time and input, even if the feedback is tough. Simple phrases like 'I appreciate you pointing that out' help demonstrate openness.

R Reflect: Take a moment to reflect on the feedback. You don't need to respond immediately with an action. Consider the feedback. This step prevents emotional reactions and helps with thoughtful decision-making.

E Engage: Engage by outlining how you will address or consider the feedback going forward. This keeps the conversation constructive and forward-thinking.

Sometimes, these simple approaches can help teams get better at starting to have the conversations that will help them be more effective and increase hope.

The middle way realistic optimism

Having explored the extremes of 'doom and gloom' and 'toxic positivity' we now come to the middle way, realistic optimism, which does build hope.

My research findings

Hope requires people to believe in a better future, and there appear to be many dangers associated with being too positive about a future that is uncertain. One participant talked about positivity in the face of uncertainty, commenting 'I suppose that's not false hope, is it? That's just hope that doesn't realise itself yet'. Another struck the balance between 'doom and gloom' and 'toxic positivity', stating 'hope is about a realistic optimism'.

Most participants talked about the balance of the positive and the negative. One talked about many aspects of this, saying:

> 'I definitely resonate with the "things are going to be better"… I have to have a picture of what's going to be. If where you want to be or you hope you're going to be is different, that's never going to be straightforward anyway because you're going to go through all those change things and all those things that are really tricky and you're going to see behaviours and things that are hard… There's an acceptance that if you want to get to that better position and you hope and believe you can get to that better position, you're going to go through a rocky road.'

Another described previous difficult experiences in helping them find a middle ground; 'There's a realism to my hope, is what I'm trying to say, that perhaps wasn't there many years ago. And that, that's really

important as well, because that keeps you safe…
I always say "full of hope, but not expectation'".
That's my fallback saying now to people. I'm always
full of hope. I'm careful with expectation'. They
further talked about the power of focusing on
positive outcomes but with an acknowledgement of
challenges, saying 'if we can stand in the truth of the
challenges, we can really make some headway with
this stuff'.

Realistic optimism in practice

Whilst leaders often choose between the extremes
and make a decision whether to go doom and
gloom or toxic positivity, I believe we need to
embrace what Tom Peters described as 'the power of
the and' rather than 'the tyranny of the or'. Should
we be really positive and keep people focused on a
better future? Yes! Should we be honest about the
challenges that could stop that happening and talk
about those 'concerns'? Also, yes! People want hope,
not hype!

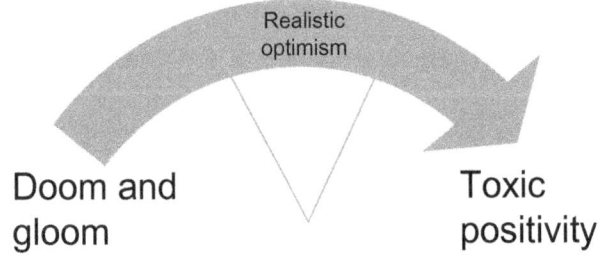

Figure 6 Realistic optimism

Embracing the 'and' of both means that we don't have to tone our message down, we can go for it in presenting a positive picture whilst being honest about the situation.

As well as balancing both positivity and negativity, I believe there are three key success factors in leading with realistic optimism. Let's imagine a scenario that helps us explore both of these factors. Imagine you need to lead a massive organizational transformation to help the organization survive in challenging times. You need to deliver a message that is both honest and hopeful. You acknowledge the challenges ahead, yet you assure your team that together, you'll find a way through. This is the essence of realistic optimism – a balance between acknowledging difficulties and inspiring hope. Imagine you've got all of the staff, a few hundred people, together in one room. You've used realistic optimism and painted a really balanced and nuanced picture and the floor is opened to discussion. And you are met with what feels like a barrage of negativity. What went wrong? What can you do? What could you have done differently?

Let's explore the three key factors that leaders need to be aware of to help in spreading realistic optimism.

1 Remember that we're making this journey at different times

As a leader, it's easy to perceive challenges as criticisms, especially when you've been working on a change initiative for some time. You might have already processed your own doubts and reached a positive outlook. However, for your team, this is new territory. They will have questions and concerns when they hear about something for the first time. I've made this mistake a few times as a leader before learning the lesson! Sometimes there needs to be a high degree of confidentiality around a change, especially if it is large-scale, commercially sensitive, or involves a merger, acquisition, or demerger.

In this situation, you might be seeking to inspire hope about a totally new scenario that nobody else saw coming. You share your vision with excitement then get floored by the negative response. The key thing to remember here is that you are further ahead on the change journey than others. You might have been on it for months and now people are hearing about it for the first time.

Elizabeth Kubler-Ross's grief curve is often referenced in this context, but I think William Bridges work on transition is much more helpful. Bridges explores how people's productivity (and I believe, their hope) will dip during the transition

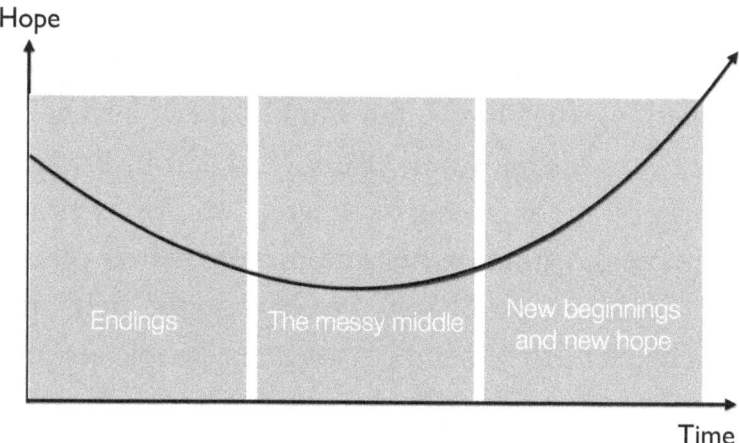

Figure 7 *Hope transition model*

before eventually being higher than it was before. Figure 7 shows my Hope Transition Model, based on Bridges' Transition Model.

When we announce a change, we start with a situation where there is already hope but as we go through the messy middle of change, hope often takes a dip. But as we reach new beginnings and new hope, we find that hope is higher than it was before and continues to grow. However, that hope dip can feel really frustrating as a leader. We can do things to flatten the curve and accelerate the process (such as great communication and listening) but the dip is still there because we are on this journey at different times. I've made this mistake as a leader on a few occasions where I've been full of hope and have been absolutely dismayed by the reception to my vision. And I've been on the receiving end of it too, where a leader has excitedly announced something that has, quite frankly, made my heart sink. As a leader, I now use my version of Bridges' transition model to notice where I am. In my head, I plot my position on this and imagine where others are. So, often, we'll be off the chart on the right and this helps us to remember that other people are just entering on the left. That knowledge hopefully gives us some empathy and, especially, patience.

2 Be aware of the risk of emotional contagion

Your goal is to inspire hope because hope is crucial for navigating the unknown. However, as you open the floor for questions, the room fills with concerns and doubts. This is where emotional contagion comes into play. Just like a cold, negative emotions can spread rapidly, overshadowing the positive message you intended to convey. The challenge is to manage this negativity without stifling legitimate concerns.

One effective strategy to combat emotional contagion is to break down the discussion into smaller groups. After delivering the main announcement, allow team members to voice their concerns in smaller groups or separate smaller meetings. This approach not only prevents negativity from dominating the conversation but also ensures that every voice is heard. By capturing these concerns and using them to build a risk register, you can address potential issues proactively. This method may seem time-consuming, but it is incredibly powerful in maintaining a hopeful atmosphere while embracing challenges.

Do you want to keep things positive or embrace concerns? And not or. Yes please. Both!

3 Keep reframing the concerns as positives

The key is to view these not as obstacles but as opportunities to enhance the likelihood of success. By anticipating potential problems and preparing to address them, you not only build hope but also increase the chances of a successful transition.

One really powerful technique that I have used many times is Daniel Kahneman's pre-mortem.[40] I've used this on lots of occasions and I'll run it like this for the group:

- I know we're being positive and full of hope but I want us to be negative for a moment and to embrace the negative so we can increase the likelihood of success and increase our hope.

---

[40] Kahneman, D. (2011). *Thinking, Fast and Slow*. Farrar, Straus and Giroux.

- Imagine we're back in this room in a few months' time and things haven't worked out and we're reflecting on why it didn't work.
- Can you please write down a list of reasons it didn't work or excuses that we'd give.
- Excellent! Now, for each reason or excuse, can you identify and write down what we can do now to ensure that doesn't happen.
- Let's consolidate those things so we have plan to increase our hope and increase the likelihood of success.

The exercise needs framing properly but it always produces valuable insight and keeps us from straying into toxic positivity. Often it produces actionable insights:

- The risk is we didn't mandate the change and close down the alternative. Action: measure this and make sure somebody is accountable for closing the alternative.
- Some leaders didn't embrace the change. Action: hold all leaders accountable for this.
- We got distracted and didn't make enough time to drive the change. Action: carve out and protect time for this. Maybe hold each other accountable. Identify and deal with (de-prioritize) things that get in the way.

Building hope through realistic optimism requires a delicate balance. It's about acknowledging the difficulties while fostering a hopeful outlook. By addressing concerns in smaller groups and reframing challenges as opportunities, you can prevent emotional contagion and maintain a positive atmosphere. Remember, every question and concern is a chance to strengthen your initiative.

From insights (on realistic optimism) to hope

Summary of key points

Hope requires us to focus on a positive future, but not to be naively positive. Doom and gloom doesn't inspire hope.

1 Don't get caught up in the deficit discourse of only pointing out what is wrong.
2 Don't just get caught up in the problems, focus on a positive future outcome.
3 Even in the most seemingly hopeless situations, there is hope to be found.

4 Even at rock bottom, we can find hope but we might have to be creative.

5 Be careful about over-emphasizing 'the burning platform' and focusing on how bad things are.

Toxic positivity doesn't inspire hope.

1 Just because some positivity is good, it doesn't mean that more is better.

2 Naive optimism just sets people up for disappointment. There might be a short-term boost in hope, but that is likely followed by a slump in hope.

3 False hope destroys trust and has a similar effect to naive optimism.

4 Where challenges are ignored and suppressed, people lose hope.

5 We need cultures of psychological safety where people can try, fail, learn, and challenge.

6 Sometimes you need to show your working out so people can believe things are possible.

7 Share and amplify the successes but don't gaslight people by pretending the challenges don't exist.

8   Where there are challenges, deal with them and don't be tokenistic. Sticking plasters don't usually build hope.

Realistic optimism builds hope.

- Realistic optimism is the middle ground that embraces the positive and negative.
- We sometimes need to acknowledge the rocky road that will take us to a better future.
- We need to stand in the truth of the challenges if we are to have hope.
- Remember that people can at different stages in their own change journey.
- Be mindful of emotional contagion where negativity can spread like a virus.
- Lean into the negatives and the challenges. If you deal with them, then they are positives as dealing with (or navigating through or around them) increases hope.

Your key reflections

What has made you think? What do you want to think about more deeply? Where are your opportunities?

Turning key reflections into hope

- For anything you want to address, how do you hope it will be in the future?
- What are your options, all the ways that you could get there? What are the obstacles?
- Now, what's your plan?
- How are you going to keep showing up and engaging with the plan?

9

Making hope happen

Hope is a project

Through my research, I've discovered that hope is, in fact, a project, or at least that is the way that many people find it helpful to view it. This revelation was surprising at first, but upon reflection, it makes perfect sense. When we hope for something – be it a better world, a more effective organization, or a future where no child is forced to live on the street – it requires a concerted effort to turn that hope into reality.

Achieving hope is never passive. It demands coordination, hard work, and a strategic plan executed with discipline and professionalism. One of the most surprising findings from my research was the role of good project managers in fostering hope. A skilled project manager can transform hope from a mere desire into a tangible reality. They are the ones who can connect the dots, paint a clear picture of the path forward, and inspire others to join the journey.

To inspire hope in others, we must be able to articulate a clear vision of how we will achieve our goals. This often involves massive change, as I experienced during my time as a trustee and chair of the charity Retrak. Our mission was to eradicate child homelessness worldwide – a daunting task given the complex issues of family breakdowns, modern slavery, and human trafficking. Yet, by developing a theory of change, we were able to map out the steps needed to make our hope a reality.

A theory of change is a strategic framework that outlines the levers for change and the actions required to achieve a desired outcome. It is a crucial tool for aligning people around a common goal, especially when the challenge seems insurmountable. For instance, to eliminate child homelessness, we needed to address the root causes, such as educating families about the dangers of trafficking and training local police to recognize its signs. We also focused on providing support to prevent family breakdowns and reintegrating children safely back into their families.

The process of building and implementing a theory of change is integral to fostering hope. It involves examining all the elements, linking causal effects, and driving the necessary change. By doing so, we create a comprehensive map that guides us in turning hope into action. This approach not only helps us achieve our goals but also empowers others to believe in the possibility of change. NPC (New Philanthropy Capital) have some excellent resources[41] that can help guide the creation and implementation of a theory of change.

Having come up with a professional plan, don't forget to have the right people to manage the project. I've been effective as a Change Director and Programme Director, but I'm not a good Project Manager. Where needed, make sure you surround yourself with the right people who can turn hope into reality through a discipline of execution and good project management.

My research findings

When reflecting on their experiences of hope in organizations, several participants reflected on the connection between hope and aspects of project management. One shared their experience:

> 'And I guess there's a really interesting interplay with hope there, isn't there... ultimately running a project is all about hope, isn't it? I guess I've never really thought about it until I started talking about it this way, but

---

[41] www.thinknpc.org/resource-hub/ten-steps/

you know, you're starting here. You want to get to there. And all you've got between here and there is your project plan, which is where the hope is.'

Many participants referenced aspects of project management, with one talking about working with people to develop meaningful plans, one focusing on having clear goals and processes, and another focusing on how hope only exists in action, 'Hope is a really active thing, hope isn't something by itself. It's not something that happens, it's not that wishful thinking, to me you've got to do something about it'.

In the context of organizational change, one spoke on the need to sustain hope through communication, stating 'You need to communicate the vision and tell people what's happening and what's going to happen to avoid leaving people in a vacuum'.

Unrelenting focus on outcomes

Hope always has an object, an outcome that we're hoping for and I often hear this when people pitch projects; 'I'm going to launch an app that will save people time with medical appointments and improve their health outcomes', 'I'm going to redesign a service that will result in more people attending their medical appointments, reducing DNA (did not attend) rates and making better use of clinician time', 'I'm going to launch a website that will help people to be empowered and own their own journey', etc. A good pitch always included what they're going to tangibly deliver as well as the outcome they're hoping for. But so often, projects get bogged down and limp over the line and deliver the service or the website or the app and don't actually deliver the outcome they promised, the hope that they promised.

Many years ago, I worked for a few years as a Benefits Management Consultant reviewing projects to see if they had delivered the impact they promised and – usually – identifying what they hadn't done and creating a plan to realize the benefits. Often I'd be called in to review a project where the delivery team were proud that they had delivered what they promised but the client didn't want to pay for as they weren't getting the outcomes they hoped for. It was a very rewarding job because the teams had mostly done 90% of the work, and it just needed a concerted effort to unlock the latent value. The problem was that they would deliver the 'thing' but not the outcome, and when business cases were being approved the organization was buying into the hope of an outcome. A key part of hope is always keeping focused on the ultimate object of our hope and making that happen. Projects often fall short in the final sprint.

I won't repeat what we've already covered in Chapter 5, but don't forget the importance of keeping your eyes on the prize. When we are talking about hope as an individual, there are lots of opportunities to get distracted. When we make this a team or organizational game, there are even more opportunities for distraction and becoming performative. Keep your eyes firmly fixed on the prize and help others to do the same.

The excellent book *Will it Make the Boat Go Faster?*[42] tells the story of an Olympic rowing team and how they transformed from dysfunctional to a winning team by having the unifying question 'Will it make the boat go faster?'. I'm always struck by the simplicity of their approach, but it demonstrates the power of an unrelenting focus on outcomes.

My research findings

Participants spoke of the need for a focus on positive outcomes, not just at the start but to maintain that focus throughout the journey. One posited the concept of a hope curve:

---

[42] Beveridge, H., & Hunt-Davis, B. (2020). *Will It Make the Boat Go Faster?* Troubador Publishing Ltd.

'Well, I think there's probably something a little bit like the change curve that you go through. Maybe there's a hope curve. There's that sort of initial "yeah, it'll be fine" then you talk to people and you realize kind of the scale of some of the challenges and you know, you have to start sort of going well, OK. We can tackle this relatively quickly and get some traction on that. You know, we can make a start on this, but that's gonna take longer and there's some big hairy stuff that we might just park for now. And, you know, we'll come back to when we've made some of the early kind of quick wins.'

One participant spoke of the importance of goals and vision, noting 'in terms of hope, I think for me it's about trying to provide a clear vision as to, OK, so this is our mission, this is where we're trying to get to' and another focused on the importance of engagement, saying 'I wanted people to feel the goal... I wanted people to have the sense of, like, why are we doing? Why are we working really hard?'

Even where plans deviated from the original, participants talked about maintaining a focus on the positive outcome, even if it was difficult and other things had changed. One shared an example where the timescales had extended significantly, but hope still remained, sharing 'I still believe it's just, it's going to take us twice as long', with another talking about hope as a sustaining force that supported progress towards a positive outcome. One participant talked about the importance of looking for the light at the end of the tunnel, saying:

> 'and just seeing the light at the end of the tunnel... because light at the end of the tunnel isn't all about life and death and doom and gloom... It's about being on a journey and seeing that you can actually see the destination. And if you're walking through a long tunnel and it's dark and, you can actually you can see where the end is, you know you're going to get there'.

Many participants shared examples where the focus on a positive outcome was usually provided by either themselves or other 'positive' people in the team. One emphasized 'there's something about having that positive personality... having some key people with that in the room at any given time' and another shared how they were able to provide that to their teams, saying 'I always try and help them focus on a positive outcome'.

Whilst most participants spoke about sharing the whole vision all at once, one spoke of the dangers of overwhelming people – 'If you hit everybody with everything all at once, that's when your hope turns into hopeless' – and spoke of breaking things down and the importance of 'Consistency, and a consistency of message, consistency of approach'.

Celebrate successes and engage with setbacks

In Chapter 5, we started to explore the importance of measuring the right things. That's true for us individually, and is even more important in teams and organizations. As we've explored several times, it is easy to get caught up in the deficit discourse and focus on what's wrong. When we're moving towards something big and bold and ambitious that we hope for, it can take time and there will be setbacks and mistakes along the way. If I reflect on my own Everesting training, the end goal always feels massive and scary and far away and if I'm not careful where I focus, I can see more setbacks and frustrations than I can progress. But the massive progress is there, I just need to remember to look for it. We need to look for and celebrate the successes, to pause and look at how far we've come.

Setbacks are inevitable and the path to hope is rarely linear. Along the way some of those setbacks might be significant and they might be mistakes or failures. How we deal with them can be vital to whether we can make hope happen. If we let setbacks dent our confidence then we are unlikely to make as much progress, and significant failures can bring hope to a grinding halt. There is one powerful way to deal with this and it is the mindset of 'we succeed or learn'. Every day, with every single step we succeed or learn. Viewing failure as learning (as with psychological safety) means that we don't cover it up or let it frustrate us, rather we use it to propel us towards the outcome we hoped for. There are many famous stories of success from failure; the lubricant WD-40 so-named because of the previous 39 failures, or the Post-it note from 3M that was created from a failed project to create an adhesive, but is simply wasn't sticky enough. Dr Allan Lim of Skratch Labs talked about his business journey,[43] noting that they had to 'make mistakes fast enough and above the water line' so that it didn't sink them. Setbacks are consistently part of the journey to hope.

For all the high-profile examples, there are millions of smaller ones. We succeed or learn. Everything moves us forward towards hope, provided that we choose to see it that way.

In cognitive behavioural coaching, we sometimes say that it isn't so much the events that happen to

---

[43] https://podcasts.apple.com/gb/podcast/bonus-skratch-labs-founder-dr-allen-lim-on-the/id1758825060?i=1000704581213

us that cause us the problems, it is the meaning that we attach to them that causes problems. Whilst there can be horrible situations where this does not apply, in most situations we can improve things by telling ourselves a more helpful and empowering story. The stories we tell ourselves are powerful and can certainty help deal with 'failure' and 'setbacks'. We get to choose the narrative. Losing is learning. Failure is feedback. Viewing it that way helps to sustain hope.

My research findings

All participants spoke about the importance of celebrating successes, of seeing results, whether that was a glimmer of hope or the outcome that was hoped for. Participants working in healthcare talked about how their hope was increased when they saw patients recovering, or even showing some small signs of improvement. Another commented 'hope certainly expanded from when we started seeing proposed improvements coming in', sharing a sense of momentum. Quick wins were one common strategy to sustain hope, with one participant reflecting on intentionally identifying them 'there was some stuff I thought we could kind of fairly quickly deal with' and another spoke of how seeing signs of making a difference – 'People's hope in what they are doing is making a difference' – would reinforce hope.

There was significant mention of the importance of how to deal with failure and setbacks. One participant said 'I think that is probably the number one thing that's given people a sense of hope is that whatever happens, we'll deal with it together and it won't get dumped on you' and spoke of their personal openness to this – 'if they're coming to me with super bad news, I'm not going to jump up and down'. Another used a military expression in describing their role in 'providing air cover' for the team, ensuring that it was safe for the team to make mistakes without punishment. Similarly, another's approach with their team was to say 'I've got your back. We'll work through it'. One participant reflected on their personal experience of being in a role where challenges were embraced and dealt with positively, and how this had enhanced their capability and their resilience. Another expressed a similarly positive view of dealing with setbacks and failure, saying 'Honestly, truly know that's just a part of the learning journey, that's part of the experience, isn't it? We learn through the failures, don't we?'.

One participant summed up the balanced view of successes and failures, saying:

'I think having that for me to maintain hope within an organization, you have to communicate, you have to be transparent, you have to be consistent, you have to acknowledge when there's been a change in direction or a failure but also a success.'

Hope is a team game

Hope is not a solo endeavour. While we can certainly nurture hope within ourselves, its true potential is unlocked when it becomes a collective effort. The power of a team is immense, and my research consistently highlights the transformative impact of camaraderie. When we unite with others, hope scales exponentially, creating a force that can drive us toward our goals.

I've already talked about the importance of intentionally surrounding ourselves with a supportive network – a cheerleading squad. Finding our tribe, those who encourage and uplift us, is crucial. However, in many organizations, the team is already in place. The challenge lies in harnessing its full potential. Teams can sometimes lose focus, become dysfunctional, or get bogged down in negative discourse. It's essential to shift our mindset and focus on how we can support and inspire one another.

Agile methodologies offer a practical approach to fostering team camaraderie. Daily huddles, with their simple agendas, provide a platform for team members to check in, share accomplishments, and discuss challenges. These gatherings create an open environment where successes are celebrated, and obstacles are tackled collectively. I've witnessed the effectiveness of these daily huddles and sprints in inspiring hope and driving progress.

Sports teams exemplify the essence of camaraderie. Picture two tennis players, exchanging fist bumps after every point, win or lose. This display of support and celebration is a testament to the power of teamwork. I've had the privilege of watching the Davis Cup live, where coaches sit beside their teams, offering simple (and powerful) encouragement: 'Go on. You've got this'. This unwavering support is vital in sustaining and building hope. To keep saying 'You've got this' seemed to work for many of the teams I watched.

Team camaraderie is a powerful catalyst for hope. By fostering an environment of support, celebration, and open communication, we can unlock the full potential of our teams. Whether in sports or the workplace, the message is simple: Together, we've got this.

My research findings

There was extensive discussion relating to this topic, more so than any other.

One participant said 'When other people do inspirational things... that fills me with hope', commenting on the inspiration that other people can bring to us, and another reflected on the importance of being heard and understood, noting 'there was a huge sense of support and camaraderie and we're in this together'. One noted that it is not unusual to have a crisis of hope and that having 'a circle of trust' of other people can address that, where you have a network where you can share anything.

One participant commented on the power of teams working through challenges together rather than in isolation – 'a sense of team, that we all work together' – and further expanded on the power of this camaraderie:

> 'you have that kind of camaraderie. We all went about it in the same way, which was not to kind of walk around miserable and it's hopeless but to just keep fighting and keep working to keep the thing going in the hope that something might turn around. And it did.'

These relational aspects were reinforced by another:

'Hope relies quite heavily on human interaction, discussion, openness, honesty, understanding what's going to inspire and drive someone... Hope was increased when people started talking to each other.'

As well as noting the power of the team in hope – 'it's what can we do as a group or as a small team to make that situation better because generally we can make it better. 'It's in our gift' and 'that hope and belief that it would be okay, really grew because actually I wasn't doing it by myself and we had a way of easing the load', one participant specifically singled out one person who they said 'saved my life in a lot of respects'. The power of these relationships was discussed by another who talked about how we can all have an occasional bad day but that 'we can lift each other up', sharing challenges that were eased because of the team they felt 'I can talk to you about it... I can process this together. I'm not doing it on my own'. One participant noted the challenges of these conversations – 'For me, while it's sometimes exhausting afterwards, for me it helps' – alongside the value they bring.

One participant discussed the ripple effect of positive relationships, sharing how other people had helped them as well as acknowledging how their own journey of hope had helped other people. Another reinforced this when they spoke of the power of storytelling and the ability to say 'look, I've been here and now I'm here. It's entirely possible'. One talked about the power of

> 'The person who stays hopeful when everyone else around [struggles]… there are icons and heroes. It's incredibly difficult to sustain that hope if you've not got others around you who are able to sustain that hope with you, or pick it up on the days when you're not feeling it.'

One participant also spoke of the power of camaraderie, but specifically mentioned the importance of diversity and inclusion, observing 'that is so important, isn't it? That you can see yourself in that piece of hope'.

From insights (on making hope happen) to hope

Summary of key points

Hope requires lots of activities to happen to help us achieve a better future and can be viewed as a project. We need to come up with a good plan and then deliver on that plan.

Hope is a project.

1 Consider having a comprehensive project plan.
2 Think about developing a theory of change so you can 'join the dots' of all that needs to be done to make hope happen.
3 Employ a good project manager.

Hope requires an unrelenting focus on outcomes.

1 Keep your eyes on the prize and help others to do the same.
2 Be aware of keeping this focus, especially if you go through the dip of the 'hope curve'.
3 Really bring the outcomes alive for people.
4 Even if everything changes, still keep the focus on a positive outcome.

Celebrate successes and engage with setbacks.

1 Make it safe for the team to try, fail, and be open about things.

2 Sometimes there will be mere glimmers of hope, but look for them and magnify them.

3 Be mindful of the motivating effect of quick wins. They can build hope.

4 Celebrate every success.

5 Embrace every challenge or failure. Deal with it and learn. Make sure that the stories you tell yourself and others are empowering.

Hope is a team game.

1 Camaraderie inspires. Hope can come from seeing other people succeed and from having a circle of trust of other people who can pick you up and build you up.

2 Teams can achieve much more than individuals can.

3 There can be a positive ripple effect of hope across a team. Feed it.

4 Diverse teams are even better.

Your key reflections

What has made you think? What do you want to think about more deeply? Where are your opportunities?

Turning key reflections into hope

- For anything you want to address, how do you hope it will be in the future?
- What are your options, all the ways that you could get there? What are the obstacles?
- Now, what's your plan?
- How are you going to keep showing up and engaging with the plan?

10

Other factors to consider in building hope

Hope is a powerful force that can drive individuals and organizations toward a brighter future. While it may not be the central focus of my research, I've discovered several fascinating dimensions of hope that are worth exploring. These insights can serve as a valuable checklist for leaders who wish to inspire and motivate others. Let's briefly explore these dimensions and uncover how they can shape our leadership approach.

Values alignment: the foundation of trust

One of the most intriguing aspects of hope is how it intertwines with values alignment. When leaders share their vision for the future, whether in a commercial or political context, people often evaluate the message through the lens of their own values. This process helps them decide whether to embrace hope and trust the leader's intentions. As leaders, it's crucial to be transparent about our values and demonstrate integrity in our actions. Our values are communicated not just through words, but also through what we do, what we tolerate, and what we celebrate. Consistency in our values builds trust and encourages others to align their hopes with our vision.

Glimmers of hope: finding light in the darkness

In challenging situations, hope can sometimes feel elusive. However, even the smallest glimmers of hope can provide a powerful message that things might be working in our favour. These tiny signs can be easy to overlook amidst the noise of everyday life, but they hold immense value. As leaders, we must actively seek out these glimmers and amplify them. By pointing them out to others and fanning the flames of hope, we can inspire those around us to persevere and remain optimistic, even in the face of adversity.

Hope as a trait: embracing individual differences

Some people are naturally more hopeful and optimistic, while others may have a different starting point. Recognizing these differences is essential for fostering a supportive environment. While hope can be a natural trait, it is also a cognitive process that can be cultivated. By understanding that everyone has a unique default position, we can work to moderate and enhance hope within ourselves and others. Embracing these differences allows us to create a more inclusive and hopeful community.

Moonshots: embracing the challenge of the impossible

Moonshots represent the pursuit of seemingly impossible goals with a high risk of failure. Whether it's a groundbreaking startup idea or a revolutionary project, moonshots require a unique approach to hope. Leaders must be prepared to handle setbacks and failures with resilience. Not all failures are created equal, and learning from them is crucial. By maintaining hope and focusing on the potential for world-changing success, we can navigate the challenges of moonshots with determination and optimism.

Coaching is hope

A common theme emerging from my research is that coaching is hope. I don't mean the finding that coaching helps as part of the overall process, but a much more fundamental finding that coaching simply helps people find hope. On reflection, it makes sense. We can't force people to have hope, we can't make them have it, or 'give' it to them but we can help them to find it. Given the connection to goal-setting, I can see the connection. I've always believed that managers need some level of coaching skills in their toolkit as they are managing people who are different to them and coaching is the only way of helping people grow (as they aren't a clone of the manager). This provides another good reason for managers to develop some level of coaching skills and is a good reminder that coaching is a great tool for developing hope.

In my own experience, the Hope Playsheet can be used as a valuable coaching tool to support people in finding their own path.

11

Stories of hope

I believe that our hope for the future comes from our hope and our actions today, so I want to share some stories of hope.

My personal hope journeys

I try to 'practice what I preach' mostly because if I believe I have something that will help people, why wouldn't I want to benefit from that myself? I want to close the book by sharing and reflecting on some of my hope journeys. Hope has cropped up throughout my life. When I graduated with an immense sense of pride as the first person in my family to go to university, the ceremony was in Liverpool's Anglican Cathedral. On Hope Street! When I watch Liverpool play, I feel emotional when I sing 'Walk on, walk on, with hope in your heart. And you'll never walk alone'. I served for several years on the board of Hope for Justice. Even when I'm watching TV (I'm a big Star Wars fan), I could be watching 'A

New Hope' where hope is a recurring theme and the Rebel Alliance makes it clear that rebellions are built on hope. I see hope everywhere. My academic work keeps being drawn back to hope, and I've found it to be an incredibly empowering lens for my work with clients both in one-to-one coaching and in running workshops on building hope. And hope has helped me in so many ways and has been there even when I didn't realize it.

Kingfisher Coaching Ltd

My career started with a very strong IT focus. With a degree in Applied Statistics and Computing, I embarked on a career in 'digital' with roles as a developer, systems analyst, project manager, and many more. I soon realized that I was much more interested in people than I was in technology, even though am I still a complete geek and love technology. It is just that I love (and am endlessly fascinated by) people even more. I started to shift my career towards change roles, trained as a coach, and got involved in some learning and development (L&D) activities. I knew what I wanted to do but that role didn't exist within the company so, in 2009, I took a leap of hope and left my job (and salary!) and set up Kingfisher Coaching. It hasn't always been an easy journey, but I had hope and I had a vision of how

I wanted it to be. And here I am 16 years later, still doing it. I feel incredibly fortunate that I get paid to do something that I care deeply about and enjoy and I get to work with some of the biggest brands in the world. Leaving full-time employment felt absolutely terrifying at the time but it is one of the best things I ever did and it is hope that got me here.

Connecting HR Manchester

I remember traveling from Manchester to London for an event and meeting people like Damiana Casile and Ryan Cheyne who, I soon discovered, lived and worked really close to me 'up north'. It felt strange that we had to travel a couple of hundred miles to meet each other and it got us talking and thinking. Subsequently, we'd often meet up at HR events where my favourite bit was the coffee break where I'd get to speak to the other attendees.

So, we had what felt like a crazy idea to launch 'Connecting HR Manchester', something that would just bring people together. We badged it as a 'tweetup' as the idea formed from the knowledge that there was a strong community of people who worked in HR, it is just that most of us hadn't met each other IRL (in real life). Damiana and I booked a space in the corner of a champagne bar, and worked hard to get the word out that the event was happening. It was terrifying. I still remember sitting there with Damiana agreeing that there were two of us and that would class as a success even if we just got to have a nice chat over a glass of champagne. And then another person turned up. And another, and then loads more. And the room was packed full of people who had great conversations. Connecting HR Manchester turned into a regular event (typically just three to four times a year) and has helped people find jobs and forge amazing connections and friendships. During Covid, it became ever more powerful and I ran it as an online event every week. Damiana moved countries and I lost a little bit of momentum but we now have an amazing team of people (I'm looking at you Alastair Swindlehurst, George Whalley, Ryan Cheyne, Vanessa Jackson, and Vicki Jackson) who work together to make this happen. What started as an idea which subsequently terrified me is now a real impactful thing. That's hope.

Connecting HR Africa

If Connecting HR Manchester tested my hope, it was nothing compared to Connecting HR Africa! I had been in Ethiopia with Hope for Justice and I was travelling back to the UK and reflecting on the experience. I had been massively struck by the hopefulness of the people that we had been working with. Many of them were in incredibly difficult situations and had very little but they were hopeful and amazingly resourceful in making the most of what they had. I really wanted to do more to support the work of Hope for Justice and – inspired by the people we worked with – I was reflecting on how I could be more hopeful and resourceful. My mind turned to Connecting HR Manchester, this amazing network that myself and Damiana Casile had created. As I reflected further, I came up with the idea for 'Connecting HR Africa' a skills-based volunteering trip where people who work in HR and L&D would visit Hope for Justice in either Uganda or Ethiopia, would pay for their own travel costs, would fundraise to further support the work of Hope for Justice, and would use their professional skills to support the staff of Hope for Justice as well as experiencing the work, and learning lots themselves.

It felt like a crazy idea and took lots of pushing to make it happen, but it happened. Hope was put into action, and we've taken teams of people to both Uganda and Ethiopia on several trips and are planning another trip to Ethiopia this year. Connecting HR Africa has raised a lot of money for Hope for Justice, has made a positive impact on many staff, and has changed the lives of many of the participants. I've felt overwhelmed (in a very good way) as I've listened to the stories from the HR professionals who have been on these trips. Going from a crazy 'I wonder if we could...?' to making this a thing wasn't easy or straightforward, but it was hope that made it happen.

Retrak and Hope for Justice

I've already mentioned these two charities several times. I was fortunate to be a Trustee and then Chair of Retrak, a charity who existed to ensure that 'no child was forced to live on the street'. Given that child homelessness is a massive problem in many countries, their work was vital. We then joined the 'Hope for Justice' family as Hope for Justice was working to eliminate modern slavery and human trafficking around the world, so there was a connection between the missions and a strong alignment of values. After the merger was concluded, I was invited to join the Hope for Justice Board, which I did and served as a Trustee for another few years.

Modern slavery is a huge criminal enterprise and makes £185 billion each year for traffickers. People might be trafficked for sexual exploitation, forced labour, domestic servitude, criminal exploitation, or forced marriage. Hope for Justice runs anti-trafficking projects in the UK, the USA, Ethiopia, and Uganda, working directly with victims and survivors, and their community initiatives help to prevent modern slavery happening in the first place.

When I look at the scale of the challenge, the problem appears to be off-the-scale overwhelming and impossible to do anything about. But Hope for Justice does do something about it. I believe that Hope for Justice would be worthwhile as an organization even if it just helped one person. But, they actually make a big positive impact on tens of thousands of lives each and every year, and that has a large ripple effect. I've been fortunate to see the work of Hope for Justice with my own eyes and it truly does bring me hope that things can change.

Everesting

I mentioned my Everesting cycling challenge in Chapter 2, where I am training to indoor cycle the height of Everest (29,029 feet) in a day. If you want to get a sense of how that height feels, I've found that I notice it when I'm flying abroad and I realize how long it takes a plane to get to that height. The thought overwhelms me. Mark Cavendish (the now-retired professional road racing cyclist) who won 35 Tour de France stages in his career did the exact same challenge in 2020, completing it in 10 hours 37 minutes and describing it as 'grim' and saying 'I take my hat off to anyone who's completed it in any capacity'.

It might sound stupid but I set my eyes on Everesting after I'd just broken all three major bones in my ankle and knew it would be months before I could walk again and I'd have to rebuild a lot of muscle. But I do like a challenge! To give you the context, I am not – and have never been – an elite athlete. At my fittest in my thirties I could run a 10km in 54 minutes but I'd then be wiped out for the rest of the day and never ever had any aspiration to run a marathon, nor the belief that I could do it. And then I hoped to complete an Everesting challenge (technically named a vEveresting when it is completed in a virtual environment indoors). I am hopeful that I will complete it in 18 hours or under. The rules allow you to take more than a day but don't allow sleep, so there's a huge incentive for me to not take more than 24 hours.

The training journey has been a real journey of hope. I mentioned in Chapter 5 that I burst into tears after managing to get on the bike (whilst still on crutches) and cycling for a whole 60 seconds! As my recovery progressed, I started training harder and eventually it was too hard as I burnt out and needed some time off the bike. But rather than give up hope, I did a hope reset and kept my eyes firmly fixed on the prize and reflected on what I had learned. Now armed with a structured training plan, I embarked on my training again but then found it too hard after a few months and realized that my lifestyle (my pace of work and lack of sleep) wasn't allowing me to train at the levels I was trying to. Another hope reset, and I managed to make a lot of changes to my life and I embarked on training again. I got much further through the training plan this time (several months) and then struggled with the volume of training. Cue another hope reset and some deep reflection and learning. By this point, if you looked at my training data you could be forgiven for concluding that I had successfully proved that I would never be able to Everest, that this pursuit was hopeless. But I know me. I know differently. The missing link was nutrition. I've joined a membership group run by a registered dietician who works with endurance and ultra-endurance athletes. It has massively changed the way I eat and fuel my workouts and – thank you Kylee Van Horn – has massively improved my training. Don't get me wrong, mindful of the origins of hope research in the science of making excuses, I found a whole host of excuses for why Everesting was never going to be for me. But embracing and considering them, helped me move beyond them.

As I write, I am two and a half weeks away from finishing a full training plan – something that I have never ever managed to do – at which point I will be doing a quarter-Everesting and starting a shorter training plan to get me to a half-Everesting and then the full one! In the whole of last year, I fell short of the height of Everest by 296 metres. This morning, I have successfully completed a challenge and ridden the height of Everest in a month.

I have come close to giving up hope on a few occasions and it has taken everything I know about hope to keep me going. I was away on holiday for a week of this challenge so I know I can Everest in three weeks. I know it will take a lot more work to be able to do it in a day but, hey, I couldn't even do it in a year and look how far I've come. And that is part of the key to this – I half expected a brass band to appear when I crossed 29,029 feet of elevation this morning but nothing happened. Well, other than an update in Strava and an email to say I was now eligible to buy an Everesting cycling jersey. I have learned and been reminded of so many things throughout this, one of which is that I need to provide the brass band! Not (necessarily) literally, but I need to pause and celebrate and make a song and dance about the successes.

When I cycle the height of Everest in a day, it will probably take me about 18 hours of cycling. It will be hope that gets me there.

Other people's stories

Demi Vollering

In Chapter 5, I mentioned how I sometimes 'borrow hope' when training on my indoor bike by watching bike races, including the Tour de France Femme avec Zwift whilst I'm riding. One that inspired me more than ever was the final stage in 2024, partly because I was riding a virtual replica of the stage as I watched the final 30 minutes of the race. Demi Vollering put in an absolutely amazing performance. Jaw-dropping and inspiring and won the final stage. I'd love to tell you that it resulted in her winning the tour, but it didn't. The honours went to Kasia Niewiadoma who – deservedly – won the overall event by just four seconds. I follow Vollering on Instagram and am always interested to hear what she says in interviews, and I always feel inspired.

On Instagram, she often uses the hashtag #ItAllStarts WithDreaming and in a recent interview,[44] she said

> 'I've always lived by "it all starts with dreaming"… Without female riders to look up to, the dream would almost disappear at times, but I'm happy I kept searching for it…

---

[44] www.theguardian.com/sport/2025/mar/26/demi-vollering-cycling-tour-de-france

Big dreams help me stay in the process. When I'm having hard times, a clear vision keeps me going. When nothing is working out, I keep fighting. I dared to dream of the biggest results and because of that they came. That's the message I want to give the world.'

That's hope, and I will continue to borrow hope from Demi Vollering.

Everybody else

I have a shortlist of about 150 stories and I can't do them justice as I think that would be a whole book in itself. You would no doubt pick a different shortlist to me, but this is who made it to the top of my list:

Malala Yousafzai who was shot by the Taliban for her advocacy for girls' education. She became the youngest Nobel Peace Prize laureate. What started with trauma, turned into a global movement.

Dame Deborah James (known to many as BowelBabe) was diagnosed with incurable bowel cancer in 2016 and died – aged 40 – in 2022. She raised millions of pounds for charity and shared her journey (in writing and in a podcast) in a way that has provided hope to so many people. Cancer Research UK sell a framed print raising funds for the BowelBabe fund, which says:

Rebellious hope is finding light in the darkness. It's choosing to remain hopeful, even when it might seem like there's nothing to be hopeful for. It's defying expectations. It's choosing to change the narrative. It's being the force to make the change.

I actually feel embarrassed including my own 'stories of hope' alongside this as they feel tiny in comparison. BowelBabe really did (and still does) inspire hope.

Nelson Mandela spent 27 years in prison and upon release, moved forward with a focus on forgiveness, peace, and reconciliation.

I won't say too much to preserve confidentiality but the staff of Hope for Justice across the world, and the survivors of modern slavery and human trafficking give me hope. The survivors that I've met are the most inspirational beacons of hope I have ever met.

I've already mentioned Victor Frankl in Chapter 2, but to survive the Holocaust and to then devote his life to helping others find hope and meaning is inspirational.

Everywhere we look, there will be people whose stories of hope inspire us. Some might involve overcoming huge trauma and some might seem minor in comparison, but all of these stories of hope can inspire us.

Conclusion

Hope is powerful at individual, team, organization, and societal levels. It propels us towards a better future. It can change lives and societies for the better, but it doesn't always come naturally and there are lots of traps we can fall into along the way.

When we choose hope, we make things better and we can start ripples of hope where hope is contagious and other people catch it. But we need to be intentional about choosing hope.

I'm absolutely not promising unicorns and rainbows but through applying my research on hope to myself, I am three stone lighter, a lot fitter, healthier, more relaxed, and making a bigger impact on the world. Hope is a strategy.

It feels like we live in challenging times where there is much conflict, what feels like an increasingly polarized world, and the worry of climate change. But we can most definitely have hope as we have a planet full of amazing people, we are more connected than ever before, and we can take advantage of more technology and innovation than ever before. I've shared lots of stories of hope, but the one for the future hasn't been written yet. We will write that story. Individually, we can be hopeful. Together, we can be exponentially more hopeful. But that will not happen by accident. It will happen through millions of us daring to dream, being hopeful, taking action, and working together to choose hope each and every day. Hope is a strategy, and realistic optimism can change the world.

Book club questions

I believe there is a power in reading together, whether it be a book club or journal club, and here are some suggested questions that you might want to consider if you're reading this as part of a book club.

- How would you define this book in one sentence?
- What did hope mean to you before reading this book?
- How would you now define hope?
- If you were going to highlight any passages in the book, what would they be?
- Who do you wish would read this book?
- Where there any surprises for you?
- What role has hope played in your life?
- How hopeful would you say you are as a person?
- If you have a role in a team or organization, what one thing from the book do you want the team or organization to know?
- What action are you going to take to build and sustain your own hope?
- What action are you going to take to help other people find and hold onto hope?
- What questions about hope do you still have after reading this book?

Acknowledgements

There are so many people I want to thank both in my hope journey and in the writing of this book, and I apologize to anyone who I remember when it is too late!

I'd like to say a huge thank you to my wife, Sue, for her unwavering support of me, and my research and writing for this book. I couldn't have done it without you and especially, like to say, thank you for turning off your 'caffeine police' role whilst I've been in the final stages of research and writing. I promise that normal service will be resumed. And I'd like to thank my family for having me grow up with 'You can't do better than your best' ringing in my ears.

In my academic research, I'd like to thank Dr Andrea Giraldez-Hayes for massive encouragement on my journey, to Dr Hanna Kampman for being an absolute beacon of hope, and to my academic research supervisors Ruth Hughes and Dr Ayse Burcin Baskurt. I am immensely grateful for all those who participated in my research, but I can't name them due to ethics and confidentiality.

I've been fortunate to work with amazing people who – although they may not even know it have really helped to build and sustain my hope in the work I do. Dr Sarah-Jane Lennie and Dr Ruth Claire Black were instrumental in encouraging me on my research journey and I've felt massively encouraged by Dr Stuart Eglin, Professor Rachel Dunscombe, Anne Cooper, and Rob Baker (whose book on job crafting filled me with hope). Sandy Lindsay has inspired me since I first started working with the company she founded (Tangerine) early in my journey, and has really helped me raise my game and be hopeful about the impact I could make. I'm immensely grateful to the amazing clients I get to work with every single day, but I need to single out Emily Wells and the NHS CXIO Network across Norfolk with whom I was able to test some early concepts around hope. Dr Gemma Dale, Kelly Swingler, and Katrina Collier are absolute machines in terms of how much research they do and how they manage to publish so many books and be out there talking about them. They inspire me and bring me hope. I'm grateful to the people I have strategic lattes with, particularly George Whalley and Alastair Swindlehurst.

I'm grateful to my best mate Keith Morrison for the encouragement along the way, for making me laugh, and for ignoring my messages when he knew I should be focused on writing. I'm also grateful to my friend Jan Malone who is fighting cancer and has put up with me turning most dog walks into a discussion on the psychology of hope.

Finally, to Alison Jones and the whole team at Practical Inspiration Publishing. I went to a writing workshop at Gladstone's Library with Alison and Bec Evans with the aim of proving to myself that I'd tried my best, given it my all, but wasn't a writer and could happily put that ambition to bed (without abandoning hope, obviously). And here we are. Thank you.

I could fill a whole book with thanks to all who have helped but you know who you are if you're part of my journey, and I am immensely grateful.

About the author

Ian started his career with a degree in Applied Statistics and Computing and spent his time working for ICI / Zeneca / AstraZeneca starting as a developer and ending up as Change Director for R&D Finance. On this journey, he realized that he was as fascinated by people as he was by technology and entered into further study in Business, Theology, and Coaching.

In 2009, Ian left his former career and founded Kingfisher Coaching, delivering leadership development workshops and coaching to help leaders find hope for themselves and those around them. He feels incredibly fortunate (not just lucky!) to be able to pay the bills doing a job he really enjoys and making an impact he cares deeply about. He firmly believes the statement 'you are enough' and enjoys holding up a positive strengths-based mirror to people so they can see what's right with them.

He is a Gallup-Certified Strengths Coach, a Fellow Member of the Association for Coaching, and a researcher in Positive Psychology with a focus on strengths and hope, and an MSc in Applied Positive Psychology and Coaching Psychology. Ian recently stepped down as a Trustee of Hope for Justice (a global charity working to end modern slavery and human trafficking) where he was also Board lead for People and Culture. He is the co-founder of Connecting HR Manchester, and founder of Connecting HR Africa (a global skills-based volunteering programme for HR professionals). Ian was named by HR Magazine in 2023 as one of 'HR's most influential thinkers'.

Ian is a scouser (born in Liverpool) who has very slowly moved along the M62 and now lives in Greater Manchester. He's married with two step-children, two grand-children, and a Border Collie called Buddy.

Bibliography

I've included lots of references throughout this book, something I always do in my writing so that: (1) you know that I'm not just making this up; and (2) you can follow the trail and explore some of the resources that pique your interest. Here's a more general bibliography about hope.

Foundational works on hope

Farran, C. J., Herth, K. A., & Popovich, J. M. (1995). *Hope and Hopelessness: Critical clinical constructs.* Sage Publications.

Groopman, J. (2004). *The Anatomy of Hope: How people prevail in the face of illness.* Random House.

Scioli, A., & Biller, H. B. (2009). *Hope in the Age of Anxiety: A guide to understanding and strengthening our most important virtue.* Oxford University Press.

Snyder, C. R. (1994). *The Psychology of Hope: You can get there from here.* Free Press.

Snyder, C. R. (2000). *Handbook of Hope: Theory, measures, and applications.* Academic Press.

Hope theory and applications

Godfrey, J. J. (1987). *A Philosophy of Human Hope.* Martinus Nijhoff Publishers.

Lopez, S. J. (2013). *Making Hope Happen: Create the future you want for yourself and others.* Atria Books.

Marcel, G. (2010). *Homo Viator: Introduction to the metaphysic of hope.* St. Augustine's Press.

Rand, K. L. (2018). 'Hope Theory: A members-only club?' In *The Oxford Handbook of Hope* (pp. 15–32). Oxford University Press.

Clinical and therapeutic applications

Cheavens, J. S., & Gum, A. (2016). *Hope Therapy: A treatment manual.* Academic Press.

Klausner, E. J. (2002). *Hope-focused Group Therapy for Depressed Older Adults.* Haworth Press.

Larsen, D. J. (2015). *Hope and Healing in Therapy: A comprehensive guide.* Routledge.

Worthington Jr, E. L. (2005). *Hope-focused Marriage Counseling: A guide to brief therapy.* InterVarsity Press.

Leadership and hope

Cameron, K. S., & Quinn, R. E. (2011). *Diagnosing and Changing Organizational Culture: Based on the competing values framework.* Jossey-Bass.

Goleman, D., Boyatzis, R., & McKee, A. (2002). *Primal Leadership: Realizing the power of emotional intelligence.* Harvard Business Review Press.

Kotter, J. P. (2008). *A Sense of Urgency.* Harvard Business Review Press.

Kouzes, J. M., & Posner, B. Z. (2016). *Learning Leadership: The five fundamentals of becoming an exemplary leader.* Wiley.

Luthans, F., & Youssef, C. M. (2007). *Psychological Capital: Developing the human competitive edge.* Oxford University Press.

Positive leadership and hope

Cameron, K. S. (2012). *Positive Leadership: Strategies for extraordinary performance.* Berrett-Koehler Publishers.

Clifton, D. O., & Buckingham, M. (2001). *Now, Discover Your Strengths.* Free Press.

Peterson, C., & Seligman, M. E. P. (2004). *Character Strengths and Virtues: A handbook and classification.* Oxford University Press.

Rath, T., & Conchie, B. (2008). *Strengths Based Leadership: Great leaders, teams, and why people follow.* Gallup Press.

Seligman, M. E. P. (2011). *Flourish: A visionary new understanding of happiness and well-being.* Free Press.

Organizational hope and leadership

Avey, J. B., Reichard, R. J., Luthans, F., & Mhatre, K. H. (2011). 'Meta-analysis of the impact of positive psychological capital on employee attitudes, behaviors, and performance'. In *Psychological Capital and Beyond* (pp. 35–52). Oxford University Press.

Cooperrider, D. L., & Whitney, D. (2005). *Appreciative Inquiry: A positive revolution in change.* Berrett-Koehler Publishers.

Ludema, J. D., Whitney, D., Mohr, B. J., & Griffin, T. J. (2003). *The Appreciative Inquiry Summit: A practitioner's guide for leading* large-scale change. Berrett-Koehler Publishers.

Youssef-Morgan, C. M., & Luthans, F. (2015). 'Psychological capital and well-being'. In *Stress and Health* (pp. 180–188). Wiley.

Transformational leadership and hope

Avolio, B. J., & Gardner, W. L. (2005). 'Authentic leadership development: Getting to the root of positive forms of leadership'. In *The Leadership Quarterly Anthology*. Elsevier.

Bass, B. M., & Riggio, R. E. (2006). *Transformational Leadership*. Psychology Press.

Burns, J. M. (2003). *Transforming Leadership: A new pursuit of happiness*. Grove Press.

Northouse, P. G. (2018). *Leadership: Theory and practice*. Sage Publications.

Hope in crisis leadership

George, B. (2003). Authentic Leadership: Rediscovering *the secrets to creating lasting value*. Jossey-Bass.

Heifetz, R. A. (1994). *Leadership Without Easy Answers*. Harvard University Press.

Heifetz, R. A., & Linsky, M. (2002). *Leadership on the Line: Staying alive through the dangers of leading*. Harvard Business Review Press.

Cultural and global leadership perspectives

Hofstede, G., Hofstede, G. J., & Minkov, M. (2010). *Cultures and Organizations: Software of the mind.* McGraw-Hill.

House, R. J., Hanges, P. J., Javidan, M., Dorfman, P. W., & Gupta, V. (2004). *Culture, Leadership, and Organizations: The GLOBE study of 62 societies.* Sage Publications.

Trompenaars, F., & Hampden-Turner, C. (2012). *Riding the Waves of Culture: Understanding diversity in global business.* McGraw-Hill.

Leadership development and hope

Center for Creative Leadership. (2017). *The Leader's Edge: Six creative competencies for navigating complex challenges.* Jossey-Bass.

Conger, J. A., & Benjamin, B. (1999). *Building Leaders: How successful companies develop the next generation.* Jossey-Bass.

Goldsmith, M., & Reiter, M. (2007). *What Got You Here Won't Get You There: How successful people become even more successful.* Hyperion.

Index

Please note that numbers in *italics* indicate illustrations, figures, or tables.

A quick word from Practical Inspiration Publishing...

We hope you found this book both practical and inspiring – that's what we aim for with every book we publish.

We publish titles on topics ranging from leadership, entrepreneurship, HR and marketing to self-development and wellbeing.

Find details of all our books at: www.practicalinspiration.com

 Did you know...

We can offer discounts on bulk sales of all our titles – ideal if you want to use them for training purposes, corporate giveaways or simply because you feel these ideas deserve to be shared with your network.

We can even produce bespoke versions of our books, for example with your organization's logo and/or a tailored foreword.

To discuss further, contact us on info@practicalinspiration.com.

 **Got an idea for a business book?**

We may be able to help. Find out about more about publishing in partnership with us at: bit.ly/PIpublishing.

Follow us on social media...

 @PIPTalking

@pip_talking

@practicalinspiration

@piptalking

Practical Inspiration Publishing